[H.A.S.C. No. 114–94]

THE CHALLENGE OF CONVENTIONAL AND HYBRID WARFARE IN THE ASIA–PACIFIC REGION: THE CHANGING NATURE OF THE SECURITY ENVIRONMENT AND ITS EFFECT ON MILITARY PLANNING

COMMITTEE ON ARMED SERVICES
HOUSE OF REPRESENTATIVES

ONE HUNDRED FOURTEENTH CONGRESS

SECOND SESSION

HEARING HELD
FEBRUARY 24, 2016

U.S. GOVERNMENT PUBLISHING OFFICE

99–625   WASHINGTON : 2017

COMMITTEE ON ARMED SERVICES

One Hundred Fourteenth Congress

WILLIAM M. "MAC" THORNBERRY, Texas, *Chairman*

WALTER B. JONES, North Carolina
J. RANDY FORBES, Virginia
JEFF MILLER, Florida
JOE WILSON, South Carolina
FRANK A. LoBIONDO, New Jersey
ROB BISHOP, Utah
MICHAEL R. TURNER, Ohio
JOHN KLINE, Minnesota
MIKE ROGERS, Alabama
TRENT FRANKS, Arizona
BILL SHUSTER, Pennsylvania
K. MICHAEL CONAWAY, Texas
DOUG LAMBORN, Colorado
ROBERT J. WITTMAN, Virginia
DUNCAN HUNTER, California
JOHN FLEMING, Louisiana
MIKE COFFMAN, Colorado
CHRISTOPHER P. GIBSON, New York
VICKY HARTZLER, Missouri
JOSEPH J. HECK, Nevada
AUSTIN SCOTT, Georgia
MO BROOKS, Alabama
RICHARD B. NUGENT, Florida
PAUL COOK, California
JIM BRIDENSTINE, Oklahoma
BRAD R. WENSTRUP, Ohio
JACKIE WALORSKI, Indiana
BRADLEY BYRNE, Alabama
SAM GRAVES, Missouri
RYAN K. ZINKE, Montana
ELISE M. STEFANIK, New York
MARTHA McSALLY, Arizona
STEPHEN KNIGHT, California
THOMAS MacARTHUR, New Jersey
STEVE RUSSELL, Oklahoma

ADAM SMITH, Washington
LORETTA SANCHEZ, California
ROBERT A. BRADY, Pennsylvania
SUSAN A. DAVIS, California JAMES
R. LANGEVIN, Rhode Island RICK
LARSEN, Washington
JIM COOPER, Tennessee
MADELEINE Z. BORDALLO, Guam
JOE COURTNEY, Connecticut
NIKI TSONGAS, Massachusetts
JOHN GARAMENDI, California
HENRY C. "HANK" JOHNSON, Jr., Georgia
JACKIE SPEIER, California
JOAQUIN CASTRO, Texas
TAMMY DUCKWORTH, Illinois
SCOTT H. PETERS, California
MARC A. VEASEY, Texas
TULSI GABBARD, Hawaii
TIMOTHY J. WALZ, Minnesota
BETO O'ROURKE, Texas
DONALD NORCROSS, New Jersey
RUBEN GALLEGO, Arizona
MARK TAKAI, Hawaii
GWEN GRAHAM, Florida
BRAD ASHFORD, Nebraska
SETH MOULTON, Massachusetts
PETE AGUILAR, California

Robert L. Simmons II, *Staff Director*
Alex Gallo, *Professional Staff Member*
William S. Johnson, *Counsel*
Britton Burkett, *Clerk*

CONTENTS

Page

STATEMENTS PRESENTED BY MEMBERS OF CONGRESS

WITNESSES

APPENDIX

THE CHALLENGE OF CONVENTIONAL AND HYBRID WARFARE IN THE ASIA–PACIFIC REGION: THE CHANGING NATURE OF THE SECURITY ENVIRONMENT AND ITS EFFECT ON MILITARY PLANNING

HOUSE OF REPRESENTATIVES,
COMMITTEE ON ARMED SERVICES,
Washington, DC, Wednesday, February 24, 2016.

The committee met, pursuant to call, at 10:03 a.m., in room 2118, Rayburn House Office Building, Hon. William M. "Mac" Thornberry (chairman of the committee) presiding.

OPENING STATEMENT OF HON. WILLIAM M. "MAC" THORNBERRY, A REPRESENTATIVE FROM TEXAS, CHAIRMAN, COMMITTEE ON ARMED SERVICES

The CHAIRMAN. The committee will come to order.

Events of recent days remind us that American national security cannot focus just on the Middle East or Africa or Europe; there are real and growing threats facing us in Asia as well. The erratic North Korean regime persistently marches toward more sophisticated nuclear weapons and longer range missiles, despite past agreements it has signed and despite pressure from China and others. Meanwhile, China is also marching steadily toward making the South China Sea a private lake, fully under Chinese control. Again, regardless of the promises made or the pressure applied, it moves ahead with its own agenda.

While we in the country are understandably alarmed at these developments, we have got to go beyond concern and decide how we will respond as we carry out our constitutional duties to raise and support, provide and maintain the military forces of the United States. The threats facing us in Asia cover a wide spectrum of military capability: from new, modern nuclear warheads that are steadily being produced by the Chinese and determined efforts by North Korea to upgrade its nuclear arsenal to missiles of increasing range and lethality to hybrid war-like tactics, which we have seen in other theaters as well.

To me, this means we must have a credible nuclear deterrent. We must have missile defense. We must have sufficient naval presence in order to deter some of what we are seeing in Asia. We also must work with key allies in the regions, strong allies, such as Japan, the Republic of Korea, Taiwan, Australia, among others. Only together can we ensure that this vital region of the world continues to be an economic engine and continue—and will have peace and stability in the future.

We are very grateful to have our witnesses today to help talk about the key role the United States military plays in achieving

(1)

those goals. Before I turn to them, I will yield to the distinguished acting ranking member, Mrs. Davis from California.

STATEMENT OF HON. SUSAN A. DAVIS, A REPRESENTATIVE FROM CALIFORNIA, COMMITTEE ON ARMED SERVICES

Mrs. DAVIS. Thank you very much, Mr. Chairman.

And if I may, I want to ask unanimous consent to submit our Ranking Member Smith's statement for the record.

The CHAIRMAN. Without objection.

[The prepared statement of Mr. Smith can be found in the Appendix on page 41.]

Mrs. DAVIS. And I also wanted to welcome Admiral Harris and General Scaparrotti and to thank you for appearing before our committee today.

The Indo-Asia-Pacific region is critical to our national interests. And despite your best efforts in promoting growth and prosperity through our committed presence and engagement, the challenges that we face, as you well know, are no small task. The North Korean regime resorts to brinkmanship and open provocation to further its objectives. North Korea's nuclear tests have openly defied the international call for a nuclear-free Korean Peninsula, and the regime uses hybrid and asymmetric warfare to reinforce its survivability and to exert undue influence.

As the chairman noted, we must work with our allies in the region to contain the North Korean regime and deter further aggression and, of course, be prepared to act if necessary. Reinforcing our missile defense posture on the peninsula in coordination with South Korea is one step in the right direction.

China continues to press its claims in the South China Sea, and their actions have shown that it too will resort to gray zone tactics short of open conflict to achieve foreign policy goals. Instead of further provocation, China should abide by internationally accepted norms and contribute to a peaceful and equitable resolution to the disputed claims.

These developments, as we all acknowledge, emphasize the need for a persistent U.S. presence. We should continue to bolster collective security, help to peacefully address concerns, facilitate productive multilateral exchanges, encourage democratization efforts, and reinforce ties with our many allies and partners.

Mr. Chairman, I look forward to our presenters today.

Thank you again very much for being here and for your great service to our country. Thank you.

The CHAIRMAN. Thank the gentlelady.

Just to remind members, immediately upon the conclusion of this open hearing, we will go to a closed classified session with our witnesses today, so if you have questions that touch on classified material, it would be best to do that later.

I am very pleased to welcome our witnesses today: Admiral Harry B. Harris, Commander, U.S. Pacific Command; and General Curtis Scaparrotti, Commander, United Nations Command, Combined Forces Command, and U.S. Forces in Korea.

Without objection, both of your written statements will be made part of the record, and feel free to summarize them or make such other comments as you would like.

Admiral Harris, thanks for being here.

STATEMENT OF ADM HARRY B. HARRIS, JR., USN, COMMANDER, U.S. PACIFIC COMMAND

Admiral HARRIS. Thank you, Chairman Thornberry and Representative Davis and distinguished members. It is an honor for me to appear before this committee. I am pleased to be here with General Scaparrotti to discuss how U.S. Pacific Command [PACOM] is protecting America's interests across the vast Indo-Asia-Pacific.

Since taking command of PACOM last May, I have had the extraordinary privilege of leading the 400,000 soldiers, sailors, airmen, marines, Coast Guardsmen, and civilians serving our Nation. These dedicated men and women and their families are doing an amazing job, and I am proud to serve alongside them.

To provide you some issues of concern, I would like to briefly highlight a few regional issues. As China continues its pattern of destabilizing militarization of the South China Sea, we have resumed our freedom of navigation operations there, a waterway vital to America's prosperity, where $5.3 trillion in trade traverses each year.

General Scaparrotti and I remain aligned in dealing with North Korea's recent underground nuclear test, followed by its ballistic missile launch.

A revanchist Russia is revitalizing its ability to execute long-range strategic patrols in the Pacific to include the basing of its newest strategic ballistic missile submarine and last month's bomber flights around Japan.

Recent terrorist attacks in Bangladesh and Indonesia underscore the fact that violent Islamic extremism is a global concern that must be crushed.

We have continued to strengthen our alliances and partnerships. Japan's peace and security legislation authorizing limited collective self-defense will take effect this year. This legislation and the revised guidelines for U.S.-Japan defense cooperation will significantly increase Japan's ability to work with us.

Thanks to the great leadership of General Scaparrotti here, South Korea and the United States have taken a strong and unified stance to maintain peace and stability on the Korean Peninsula. In the face of recent North Korean aggression, PACOM hosted a tri-CHOD [Chief of Defense] meeting between U.S. Chairman of the Joint Chiefs, General Dunford; Japan Chairman, Admiral Kawano; and South Korea Chairman, General Lee. Trilateral cooperation between Japan, South Korea, and the United States is a priority, and I am doing everything I can to enhance it.

Our alliance with the Philippines took an important step forward when the Philippine Supreme Court recently upheld the Enhanced Defense Cooperation Agreement, or EDCA, which will provide significant partnership and access benefits.

I am also excited about our growing relationship with India, where I will visit next week. As the world's two largest democracies, we are uniquely poised to help bring greater security and prosperity to the entire region.

Two visionary policies are now coinciding as the United States rebalances west to the Indo-Asia-Pacific and India implements its

"Act East" policy. Last month's Malabar exercise between India, Japan, and the United States shows the security interconnectedness of the Indian Ocean, Asia, and the Pacific Ocean.

I rely heavily on Australia, not only for its advanced military capabilities across all domains but, importantly, for Australia's warfighting experience and leadership in operations around the world.

These examples clearly demonstrate to me that the United States is a security partner of choice in the Indo-Asia-Pacific. It is also why I believe that our strategic rebalance has taken hold. Given that four of the five strategic problem sets identified by Secretary Carter—China, North Korea, Russia, and ISIL [Islamic State of Iraq and the Levant]—are in our region, I would say that we can't rebalance fast enough. But there is more work to do, and we must not lose the momentum.

So I ask this committee to support continued investment in future capabilities. I need weapons systems of increased lethality that go faster, go further, and are more survivable. If funding uncertainties continue, the U.S. will experience reduced warfighting capabilities, so I urge the Congress to repeal sequestration.

Finally, I would like to thank this committee and the whole Congress for your enduring support to PACOM and to the men and women in uniform, our civilian teammates, and our families.

Thank you. And I look forward to your questions.

[The prepared statement of Admiral Harris can be found in the Appendix on page 43.]

The CHAIRMAN. Thank you, sir.

General.

STATEMENT OF GEN CURTIS M. SCAPARROTTI, USA, COMMANDER, UNITED NATIONS COMMAND, COMBINED FORCES COMMAND, AND U.S. FORCES–KOREA

General SCAPARROTTI. Chairman Thornberry, Ranking Member Davis, and distinguished members of the committee, I am honored to testify today as the Commander of the United Nations Command, Combined Forces Command, and the United States Forces-Korea [USFK]. On behalf of the American soldiers, sailors, airmen, and marines, and our civilians serving in the Republic of Korea, thank you for your support.

Admiral Harris, thank you for your vision and the professional support of the entire PACOM team for USFK.

I have prepared brief opening remarks, and I appreciate that my written posture statement is being entered into the record.

Since my last testimony, our U.S.-ROK [Republic of Korea] alliance has continued to focus on advancing our combined capabilities. Some of these advanced capabilities include the establishment of the first U.S.-ROK combined division, additional rotations of U.S. forces to the peninsula, the execution of our annual combined training exercises, and steady progress on our $10.7 billion plan to relocate U.S. forces in Korea. Furthermore, the Republic of Korea has improved its capabilities with the recent establishment of the Korean Air and Missile Defense System and Center and the Allied Korea Joint Command and Control System.

The Republic of Korea has also invested in modern equipment, with the purchase of the F–35 Joint Strike Fighter, Global Hawk, the Patriot Advanced Capability-3 missile upgrades, and also AH–64 Apache helicopters. These alliance advances help counter the real and the proximate North Korean threat.

North Korea continues to conduct provocations and to resource its large conventional force. And, of greater significance, North Korea continues to aggressively develop nuclear weapons and ballistic missiles in direct violation of the U.N. Security Council resolutions, as demonstrated with its fourth nuclear test and its fifth TD–2 launch in January and February.

In regards to this threat, my top concern remains the potential for a North Korean provocation to start a cycle of action and counteraction which could quickly escalate, similar to what we experienced this past August. While I am proud to report that our alliance stood shoulder to shoulder and deescalated the situation, it could have spiraled out of control and demonstrates why we must remain ready to "fight tonight."

To maintain this level of readiness, we will continue to focus on sustaining, strengthening, and transforming the alliance, with an emphasis on our combined readiness in four critical areas. First, ISR [intelligence, surveillance, and reconnaissance] remains my top readiness challenge. CFC [Combined Forces Command] USFK requires additional persistent all-weather ISR capabilities, as well as dependable moving target indicator support to maintain situational awareness and provide adequate decision space.

Second, it is critical for the alliance to establish a layered and interoperable ballistic missile defense. To advance this goal in the near future, we will begin bilateral consultations regarding the feasibility of deploying the THAAD [Terminal High Altitude Area Defense] system to the Republic of Korea, which would complement the Patriot system's capabilities.

Third, we must maintain an adequate quantity of critical munitions to ensure alliance supremacy in the early days of conflict on the peninsula. This requirement is further amplified by the approaching loss of cluster munitions due to shelf-life expiration and the impending ban.

And, fourth, we must focus on command, control, communications, computers, and intelligence, or C4I. Both the United States and the Republic of Korea are investing in new tactical equipment that will comprise a reliable C4I architecture, but more is required.

In closing, I would like to express how proud I am of our service members, our civilians, and their families serving in the Republic of Korea, who never lose sight of the fact that they are serving on freedom's frontier.

I would also like to recognize Ambassador Mark Lippert, Admiral Harry Harris, and the U.S. and ROK senior leaders for their enduring commitment to our mission.

I thank you and this committee for your support, and I look forward to your questions.

[The prepared statement of General Scaparrotti can be found in the Appendix on page 67.]

The CHAIRMAN. Thank you, sir.

Let me ask you each to address really a very basic question, and that is, do you have the military forces required to fulfill the missions you have been assigned?

And, Admiral Harris, you mentioned the freedom of navigation operations, which have been underway. From what one reads, they are pretty few and far between and don't seem to be making much of a difference, because we also read that the Chinese have put surface-to-air missiles on these new islands they are constructing. So if you could address, broadly, in your theater, do you have the military forces to carry out the missions you are assigned, and then, more specifically, the Chinese South China Sea issues that have arisen.

Admiral HARRIS. Yes, sir. Happy to do that.

With regard to the first issue of do I have the forces necessary to conduct our missions, today, I feel I do. I think we are set up well in NDAA [National Defense Authorization Act] 2016. Thanks to the Congress for that. And in the budget submission for fiscal year 2017, it meets the concerns that I had in the past, the fiscal year 2017 budget addresses those concerns. So I am comfortable with where we are today, but today we are not at war, and I think that is an important point.

There are concerns that I have, clearly. As General Scaparrotti mentioned, there are concerns about munitions. My submarine numbers—and I mentioned this yesterday during my testimony— I don't have the submarines that I feel I need, but that is a function of the total number of submarines that the United States Navy has and the global demand for that platform.

More persistent intelligence, surveillance, and reconnaissance aircraft and systems, ISR, is a requirement, I think, as well as cyber and getting after cyber.

I have testified in the past and have spoken in the past about the need for a long-range anti-surface missile, a missile that can out-stick, if you will, Chinese missile systems in the Pacific and so on. And I am pleased that in the fiscal year 2017 budget, you know, there are funds put against development of LRASM, the long-range anti-surface missile. Secretary Work recently spoke about the work that has been done to improve the SM–6 missile and give it an anti-surface and anti-ship capability, which I think is dramatic, and that is exactly what I need in the Pacific.

With regard to your question about China's actions, in my opinion, China's intent to militarize the South China Sea is as certain as a traffic jam in DC. It is no doubt in my mind what their intent is. Their SSMs, their surface—their SAMs [surface-to-air missiles], rather, their missiles on Woody Island, their 10,000-foot runways that they are building in Subi Reef and Fiery Cross Reef and elsewhere, their advanced radars that we saw pictures of the last couple days at Cuarteron Reef, these are all indications of militarization. And, in my mind, they are changing the operational landscape of the South China Sea.

The CHAIRMAN. And if you could address, sir, the freedom of navigation operations. Do you have enough ships, and what kind of ships would you say are most effective for those sorts of operations?

Admiral HARRIS. Sure. So, on the freedom of navigation operations, clearly, have enough ships to do that. The 7th Fleet out there, homeported principally in Japan, has the ships, the requisite ships to do freedom of navigation operations.

The best kind of ship, in my opinion, to do that is the DDG–51-class, *Arleigh Burke*-class destroyer, highly capable, the right kind of weapons and the right kind of systems to ensure that freedom of navigation operations are conducted well and the ship is well able to defend itself should those operations go awry.

Regarding the frequency of freedom of navigation operations and their effect on China's militarization in the South China Sea, freedom of navigation operations, the military part of that, the freedom of navigation operation itself is only a part of the broader policy approach to what China's doing. So I think my part of that, the execution of the operation itself, is one piece of it, and I think we are doing that, as I said, and we will be doing more of it, as I have spoken before in other venues. We will be doing them more, and we will be doing them with greater complexity in the future. And as the Secretary said, we will fly, sail, and operate wherever international law allows. And then there is a policy piece to it and a diplomatic piece and a political piece to it, and that is for the whole-of-government effort on moving China and their position in the South China Sea.

The CHAIRMAN. General, do you have the forces you need to carry out the mission to which you have been assigned?

General SCAPARROTTI. Chairman, thank you for the question. I would say that, first of all, for the forces on the peninsula, I enjoy being financed or budgeted at the very top of the priority list, so the forces are getting the funding to do the exercises, the training, and assets that they need on the peninsula to be ready to fight tonight, and I appreciate the support of this committee in ensuring that we do have that resourcing.

As I noted in my opening comments, there are areas of concern. First is ISR. On the Korean Peninsula, we are facing a foe that is a million strong, and it is literally 35 miles from the capital and the—you know, half of their population, the Korean population, 35 miles away with an adversary that uses a cycle of provocation. So, typically, I think I have about 12 hours or less warning, and persistent ISRs allows me to have that indication and warning and to set my posture to first defend South Korea and the large American citizen population that we have there as well. So ISR is something that is at the top of my list.

I mentioned ballistic missile defense. You are well aware of the large arsenal that North Korea has in ballistic missiles that are—that is growing in strength but also in accuracy. I think that the discussions we are having right now to add THAAD to Korea are very important. We need THAAD there to have a layered defense. I need more munitions so that I have the first 30 days of munitions for the fight in terms of interceptors, and I rely on the quick deployment of at least two more battalions of Patriot as well if we go to crisis. So, you know, the assets of BMD [ballistic missile defense] there, the more that I have there, the better protected we are.

And I think those are the primary of those four that I would mention shortly here, and I can go into more detail later.

The CHAIRMAN. Thank you.

Mrs. Davis.

Mrs. DAVIS. Thank you, Mr. Chairman.

And, again, I appreciate you both being here.

I wonder if you could expand a little bit more on the South China Sea issues, obviously the militarization there, China's consolidation of its claims and rejection of internationally accepted methods of dispute. So how might we best mitigate the risk of miscalculation leading to increased tensions or even conflict in the area?

Admiral HARRIS. Well, I think, ma'am, that, short of military confrontation, which we all want to avoid, I think the way forward, the best way to go forward is to present and maintain our credible military power and to maintain our network of like-minded allies, partners, and friends in the region and encourage them to operate in the South China Sea. And we must continue to operate in the South China Sea to demonstrate that that water space—and the air above it—is international and not the territory of any nation.

I think the diplomacy, obviously, is probably the most important thing. We need to encourage China to act as a responsible actor on the international space when it comes to things like the South China Sea. Secretary Kerry recently said at Sunnylands that we have only one policy with regard to the South China Sea, and that is a negotiated settlement, that is to negotiate and work with China, and that is kind of where I am on that.

Mrs. DAVIS. Thank you, Admiral.

And, perhaps, General Scaparrotti, with your hat as well, how do we better complement, then, our efforts? Certainly you are speaking to the defense lane very appropriately here today, but I am wondering about other Federal agencies and working with them in diplomatic, economic, and certainly assistance efforts in that kind of holistic way. What are we doing? Which could we be doing more? Where are the gaps?

General SCAPARROTTI. Well, I think, you know, we know from experience that a holistic approach is always the most effective, and so I think, including Treasury, many of the other agencies here, including them in all that we do, we on—in USFK as a subcomponent command, we also have close connection to all those agencies that work with PACOM, and they are regularly a part of our planning, our exercises, in fact, the one we will do this next month. And I think that type of close collaboration with all the agencies in our government, bringing them into the planning, the exercises that we do, gives them good awareness. And then, you know, as things happen in the theater, we have a relationship, we have an understanding, and we can work and collaborate much more quickly.

Mrs. DAVIS. And do you see a greater role for Congress in this as well, since we tend to stay in our lane also?

General SCAPARROTTI. Well, I do. And I appreciate the fact that many Members of Congress come out to see us. Particularly, I know it is a long trip to Korea, but I think Korea is a place that is complex, and until you have stood on the DMZ [Demilitarized Zone], then just that picture alone is quite informative, and I appreciate the fact that so many make the trip and have the conversation and discussion with us.

Mrs. DAVIS. Yeah. Thank you.

Thank you, Mr. Chair.

The CHAIRMAN. Thank you.

Mr. Wilson.

Mr. WILSON. Thank you, Mr. Chairman.

And, Admiral, General, thank you so much for your service. I want to thank you, the service members, military families. What a commitment of protecting American families, also protecting our great allies.

And, Admiral Harris, I am particularly grateful that I have had the opportunity to visit with you in the past. And, to me, you are a living example of America's alliance with Japan. It is just, to me, so historic and inspiring to know that we have a Japanese-American as the U.S. Pacific commander at Pearl Harbor. How far we have come. And just being in your presence has just been so positive and has to be reassuring to the people all over Asia.

Also, I am very grateful that my family has had an association with Asia. My dad served in the Flying Tigers during World War II, and I grew up hearing from him a great affection for the people of China and the people of India. And so I am hopeful that indeed positive can continue to advance, but with that in mind, Admiral, I appreciate your interest in maintaining our technological superiority, and later today, there will be a subcommittee hearing of the Emerging Threats and Capabilities Subcommittee on the Department of Defense science and technology programs. These issues continue to be of crucial importance to this committee, particularly the chairman, and this is key to our warfighters' future success.

Could you please describe what do you see as the right balance between investing in future capabilities, like the third offset strategy, and getting the commander what he needs now? How has the fiscal year 2017 budget request prioritized the modernization affecting your command?

Admiral HARRIS. Thanks, sir, for those questions. I will just start by talking about General Stilwell for just a second. There is an article in today's clips about how the Chinese are honoring General Stilwell in Chongqing in China at a museum that is run by the government there, and the relationship that he formed and his feelings for the Chinese. So I think that is an appropriate way to start this off. Thank you for that.

Mr. WILSON. Absolutely.

Admiral HARRIS. With regard to the fiscal year 2017 request, it has, I think, a good mix in it of funding for what we need today and funding for technological innovations, such as the third offset. Recently, Secretary Work talked about the SCO office, the Special Capabilities Office, and the work that they are doing. And this is important stuff as we seek to not only modernize our force but also to maintain the force we have.

And so, you know, as a combatant commander, I don't have the luxury of waiting 5 years for the next great thing that is going to come down the pike, because I have to be ready to fight tonight, and that is the stance that we take in the Pacific most—epitomized by General Scaparrotti and the challenge he has on the peninsula. So, you know, I can't say to you all: Hey, just give me a 5-year break here while we wait for the next technology thing to come down the road. So I need to have a modernized, capable military today, but I recognize as a uniformed officer that we have to modernize, and so that is the challenge, I think, for the service chiefs.

You know, I talked yesterday about how much easier it is to be an insatiable combatant commander than it is to be a service chief in 2016, but as a nation, we have an insatiable need for security, and rightfully so. And so, you know, it comes to the point, I guess, in the forward forces.

So I am pleased with how my input to the Secretary was upheld in the fiscal year 2017 budget, and I am pleased that that budget not only ensures that I have a modern, capable force to fight today but that the needs that I have identified, the shortfalls that we talked about in the last question, are being addressed.

Mr. WILSON. And we look forward to your input.

And, General Scaparrotti, China and North Korea's increased utilization of hybrid warfare, are we prepared for cyber warfare potential on the Korean Peninsula?

General SCAPARROTTI. Sir, it is one of my concerns, given that North Korea has made a deliberate effort to improve their capabilities as much as they can. Kim Jong-un has stated that. And, as you know, he has demonstrated their capability with Sony and the attack on South Korea's media and banking industries in 2013. So I am very concerned about it.

I would answer your question and say, yes, I believe we are prepared today on our—you know, defense of our military systems and within the cyber domain, but it is a rapidly developing domain and area that we have to stay on it every day. We specifically have been working on our joint cyber center. I recently have been added a cyber mission team specifically for Korea, and that is building now. That is a great addition to our capability.

I would mention to you that I also have another concern, and that is that I am within an alliance, the ROK's capability and ours, so we are collaborating with their joint cyber center as well to make sure that we don't have a vulnerability because of our combined systems, et cetera, and that is work that we need to continue to do.

Mr. WILSON. Thank you.

The CHAIRMAN. Mr. Larsen.

Mr. LARSEN. Thank you.

Thank you, Mr. Chairman.

And thanks, gentlemen, for making it out.

You know, on the West Coast, it is not that far to go to Korea, so maybe, from here, it is, but it is not that far from home.

So we get a lot of questions about when North Korea does things and when China does things. First, for Admiral Harris, a couple reports have come out recently, one looking at the rebalance strategy and what can be done to improve that and enhance that. One suggestion—this is out of CSIS [Center for Strategic and International Studies]—one suggestion was a western Pacific joint task force, and I was wondering what your opinions about that are. And in the answer, if you could relate that to building partnership capabilities and whether or not, much like we do with NATO [North Atlantic Treaty Organization], there is a NATO commitment of a 2 percent of GDP [gross domestic product], but we can do that in a formal structure, if there is a value of informal commitments from our friends and allies in the region to invest in their capabilities to support regional objectives.

And then I have got a question for the general after that.

Admiral HARRIS. Yes, sir. Good to see you.

Mr. LARSEN. Good to see you.

Admiral HARRIS. On the CSIS study, I have read it, they had a number of interesting recommendations in there. I had a meeting with the CSIS leadership and spoke to them in my last trip to Washington.

On the idea of a maritime task force for the western Pacific, we have one, and it is called PACOM. And if there is some smaller entity of that, we have that also, and it is called the 7th Fleet. So I am very comfortable with the command and control structure and the forces as they are arrayed under PACOM. So there is a commander of the U.S. Pacific Fleet, which is a JTF [Joint Task Force]-certified, large combatant level staff headed up by a four-star that can carry out any operation that I need; the same with U.S. Army Pacific, General Brooks, four-star Army general, huge land forces under his command that can do that, if necessary. And then, in the far Pacific, in the Far East, you know, there is the U.S. 7th Fleet and all of its capability, there is the 3rd Marine Expeditionary Force and all of its capability. So I think that we have in existence today the thing that CSIS recommended by another name. So I am comfortable with that, but I appreciate the insights that I got from their study.

Regarding partner capabilities, we could not do what we need to do alone, and we have great allies and partners in the region. I will start with Japan and its capability: a very powerful military, a tremendous maritime self-defense force, a great submarine force, a very capable land force, and a very strong air force in Japan. And on the other end of the globe down there is Australia, a partner and ally. who has been with the United States, fought with us in virtually every conflict in the 20th century, and certainly into the 21st century. They are—they have a highly specialized, highly trained, very capable military that are completely aligned in terms of equipment and training and that with the United States. So, as I mentioned in my opening statement, I rely heavily on Australia, not only for their operational capability but for their warfighting experience and advice.

I think we will not see anything resembling NATO——

Mr. LARSEN. Right.

Admiral HARRIS [continuing]. In the Pacific. It is—each country there is so different—and they face different levels of threat; they have different levels of relationships with other countries—that I don't think we will get this large, broad multilateral alliance like NATO. But the good news is we have strong alliances with five nations in the Pacific. We have strong partnerships with a whole lot more. And we are working hard, working strongly on improving trilateral cooperation between the U.S., Japan, and Korea; between the U.S., Japan, and Australia; and the U.S., Japan, and India.

Mr. LARSEN. Okay. Yeah. I just have very few seconds left for—thank you.

General, just quickly, would the ROKs be prepared today for THAAD if there was an agreement today to deploy THAAD to the Republic of Korea, and if not, what does that timeline look like?

General SCAPARROTTI. Representative, we will have a—we are forming a joint working group that I think will have its first meeting probably within a week. I think we will have that settled. THAAD is a complex system. It is going to take some time for us to find the right location, because where you locate it makes a difference of how effective it is. So we have got to find the right location and do that work, which we will do in accordance with our SOFA [Status of Forces Agreement]. I am confident that that process will go well, but at this point, it is hard—it is difficult for me to tell you what the timeline looks like, but I should be able to do that, you know, and relatively soon.

The CHAIRMAN. Mr. Rogers.

Mr. ROGERS. Thank you, Mr. Chairman.

General Scaparrotti, I wanted to follow up on that area. Given Kim Jong-un's erratic behavior and recent nuclear tests and ballistic missile tests, what capabilities do you need to make sure you can maintain the security of your forces as well as the ROK?

General SCAPARROTTI. As I said, the most important to me is ISR, because it allows me to be in the proper posture to be able to get ahead of whatever it is he intends to do. And on the Korean Peninsula, I have got a very large conventional force in very close proximity to Seoul. That is one problem set. And then I have their asymmetric problem set, which is primarily their nuclear; their missile; their SOF [special operations] forces, the largest SOF forces in the world, 60,000 strong; long-range artillery capability; and their cyber. Many of those are deeper into the country, so it is a very difficult ISR challenge, probably one of the toughest in the world, given the terrain, mountainous.

Mr. ROGERS. Are your current ISR capabilities adequate?

General SCAPARROTTI. I need more persistence, sir. That would be very, very helpful. So that is the one I come up. And then the other four in particular that I mentioned earlier are the ones that I most need.

Mr. ROGERS. Great. Thank you.

Admiral Harris, can you please explain the advantages of ensuring that U.S. Patriot battalions have modular capability?

Admiral HARRIS. Sure. Clearly, Congressman, because of the mobility associated with that and the fact that I can move the Patriots around with some degree of flexibility. So in the Pacific, Patriot is a key part of our ballistic missile defense, as is THAAD. So we have a THAAD battery in Guam that is there on a temporary basis now, expected to go to a permanent status, PCS [permanent change of station] status, if you will, later this year, and then, as General Scaparrotti mentioned, as we work with the Koreans to consult on putting THAAD in Korea as well. Then the other part of that, of course, is Aegis, so——

Mr. ROGERS. Speaking about Aegis, my understanding is the discussion was to take the Aegis Ashore site there in Hawaii and activate it instead of just being a training facility. Now I hear there is discussion of closing it down. What is going on with——

Admiral HARRIS. Well, that—so I talked about my desire to keep it as a permanent facility, because it has demonstrated a great capability. Now, it was built as a training facility and testing facility for the Aegis Ashore sites in Europe, but I think we should study it. I think we should take a hard look at it and whether we want to make it a permanent facility or not, but there is a lot between now and then.

Mr. ROGERS. Okay.

Admiral HARRIS. This is just an idea now, but the Aegis Ashore in Hawaii, for example, has no interceptors, right. I mean, it— so——

Mr. ROGERS. Right. We would have to put them in. I agree.

Admiral HARRIS. So there is a lot there, but I think it is worthy of study, and that is kind of where we are now. So we are a long way from making a decision either way right now.

Mr. ROGERS. Great. As I read the President's budget, there are four Baseline 9 destroyers that we are losing. Were any of those going to PACOM, and if so, what is the effect of losing those destroyers?

Admiral HARRIS. I will be honest with you, I am not familiar with that number, but we are getting new Baseline 9 destroyers in Japan now; we are setting out there in part of the overseas home-porting program. So, in the Pacific, I am comfortable with where we are with regard to that capability, and that is a tremendous capability. I mean, that ties together——

Mr. ROGERS. Right.

Admiral HARRIS [continuing]. The E–2D and the Aegis system for this thing we call cooperative engagement.

Mr. ROGERS. Right.

Admiral HARRIS. So I am pleased with that.

Mr. ROGERS. What is the benefit of having an Aegis Ashore site in Japan for the U.S. and for Japan?

Admiral HARRIS. Sir, I don't know that there is a benefit to it. You know, we have—Japan has Patriot batteries, and that is—they are very capable. We have the TPY–2 radar systems at Shariki and Kasumigaseki, and those are helpful. I think there is a study in place to look at whether an Aegis Ashore site has utility in Japan, but it is premature for me to make that statement now.

Mr. ROGERS. Yeah. My understanding was it would free up our Aegis ships in the Asian Pacific. Is that not——

Admiral HARRIS. That could be, I mean, certainly.

Mr. ROGERS. Okay. Thank you, Admiral.

Thank you, Mr. Chairman.

The CHAIRMAN. Ms. Bordallo.

Ms. BORDALLO. Thank you, Mr. Chairman.

I would like to remind my colleagues that my home is next door to North Korea, when we talk about distances.

So, Admiral and General, thank you for your testimony and for your service and leadership.

Mr. Wittman and I were just out in your region a day ago, and I appreciated the opportunity to get updates on the progress we are making in realigning forces and trying to posture our force to respond to the environment in the region. One of the things that people become aware of when traveling in the region is the tyranny of distance. This is never more evident than when it comes to making sure we maintain a forward and deployed fleet.

And, Admiral, you noted the need for more submarines as a top priority yesterday. To support this, I believe it is critical that we maintain robust ship repair and dry-dock capabilities, including at a nuclear capable level, in the western Pacific.

Now, you wrote a letter to the Guam Economic Authority stating, and I quote: "The Navy has consistently stated a robust ship repair capability in Guam as a matter of strategic importance and remains an operational priority for the Pacific Fleet."

Do you continue to share this view, Admiral?

Admiral HARRIS. I do, Congresswoman.

Ms. BORDALLO. Admiral, in your testimony before the SASC [Senate Armed Services Committee] yesterday, the Japan press picked up on a 2-year delay in IOC [initial operational capability] for the Futenma Replacement Facility, and I believe this delay is due to legal challenges after the election of Governor Onaga. I just want the people of Guam to be clear about whether this delay in Okinawa would impact Guam. And, as you know, the 2012 2+2 statement delays progress on Futenma from progress on Guam. Moreover, Chairman Wittman noted in his recent visit to Guam that we were light years ahead of where progress stood several years ago. So I would note that we have made great progress. So can you comment on this progress on Guam in the coming years and the importance of the investments in military construction for Guam in this year's budget? And how does that help you as PACOM commander address the changing nature of threats in the Asia-Pacific region?

Admiral HARRIS. Yes, ma'am. I believe that Guam is a strategic bastion for the United States. The capabilities that are there and its location demand that we consider it a strategic bastion, and so, you know, we have put our fourth SSN there, nuclear submarine there, and we have brought in our second submarine tender there. So that is very exciting and I think the right level of emphasis on our submarine force in the western Pacific.

With regard to Futenma, I will defer to the Marine Corps on where they stand on the linkages between the Futenma Replacement Facility and the exodus of that group of marines from Okinawa to both Guam and Hawaii, but clearly the plan as conceived was, you know, we would move marines from Futenma to Camp Schwab-Henoko and then subsequently move a group of marines, 8,000 or so, from Okinawa to Hawaii and Guam, Guam and Hawaii in that order, but whether we are going to link that now or not, given that there is a delay in the movement of forces from Futenma to Schwab, I will have to defer to the Marine Corps on that.

Ms. BORDALLO. I just want to be clear as to whether Guam would be affected in——

Admiral HARRIS. It would only be affected perhaps in terms of timing, but the intent to move marines to Guam remains as strong as ever. That intent is there, and the resources we are putting into Guam and in the Commonwealth of Northern Marianas, that is proceeding apace.

Ms. BORDALLO. Thank you.

And I yield back, Mr. Chairman.

The CHAIRMAN. Thank you.

Mr. Wittman.

Mr. WITTMAN. Thank you, Mr. Chairman.

Gentlemen, thank you so much for your service and thank you for the great job that you are doing in the Asia-Pacific. As Ms. Bordallo said, we had a great trip there.

Admiral Harris, I want to ask your perspective. As we got the laydown on the situation there in the Asia-Pacific, one of the things that was really compelling to me was the effort by the Chinese in the South China Sea. As you pointed out, their efforts there on Woody Island and the Paracels is something that is done. There is nothing that we can do to necessarily reverse that. The place, though, where I do believe we can have an impact is in the Spratly Islands. As you know, over 3,000 acres of reclamation there, those places are set up specifically, I believe, for them to militarize those areas.

As you spoke in your opening testimony, you talked about submarines as one of the elements that you have as a critical part of force structure. There is also a suggestion of a second aircraft carrier. In looking at what we can do to deter or prevent further militarization of the South China Sea, give me your perspective on the priority that you would need as far as naval assets, and I am asking you submarines versus the second aircraft carrier. Give me what your priorities would be in that situation.

Admiral HARRIS. Thanks, Congressman.

My priority, given the way you framed the question, is clearly submarines. Submarines are the original stealth platform. They clearly give us an asymmetric advantage. Our asymmetry in terms of warfare, because of submarines, is significant. And, you know, in the modernizing sense, we need to maintain that asymmetric advantage.

The second aircraft carrier, you know, I am a combatant commander, and I want more, and I want it now, right? The more I can get it, the faster I can get it, the happier I am.

Mr. WITTMAN. Sure.

Admiral HARRIS. But I think there are fiscal, diplomatic, and political hurdles—significant ones—to overcome before we would put a second carrier strike group in the western Pacific, you know, when you talk about an air wing, where would you put it, where would you train them, the 10,000 sailors, their families, the housing, the schools, the hospitals, the whole thing. But there are other things that we could do, in my opinion, that would improve our capability in the western Pacific and have an effect. We could consider putting another SSN [attack] submarine out there. We could put additional destroyers forward. We could put maybe the new destroyer, the DDG–1000s, move them forward. So there are a lot of things we could do short of putting a full carrier strike group in the western Pacific.

Mr. WITTMAN. Very good. And you believe that is the most effective way that we could deter further militarization there in the Spratlys?

Admiral HARRIS. I think that is a big part of it——

Mr. WITTMAN. Good.

Admiral HARRIS [continuing]. Yes.

Mr. WITTMAN. Very good. Thanks, Admiral Harris.

General Scaparrotti, I appreciate your time when we were there visiting at U.S. Forces-Korea and the great job you are doing there.

One of the questions I wanted to ask is, as you look at your needs—and, as you have pointed out, the threat, ISR, a critical portion of that to make sure you can look at what potentially is happening to the north. Another element, though, that is important is, if you do need to act, is to make sure that you have not only the information and people, the manning, but also the hardware.

Give me your perspective on where you are right now as far as munitions stores and whether they are adequate for what you look at as the potential scenarios there with North Korea.

General SCAPARROTTI. Thank you, sir, for the question. As you know—I will first describe the conflict on the Korean Peninsula, because while we have seen provocation, if we went to conflict in the Korean Peninsula, given the size of the forces and the weaponry involved, this would be more akin to the Korean War and World War II: very complex, probably high casualty. And because of that, first of all, it is just going to be a situation where I want to be ahead of that and be able to deter the aggressor. So my need is particularly to have the forces, the ballistic missile defense forces, et cetera, so that when I pick up the indication and warning, I can establish my defense, protect South Korea, our forces, and our population there immediately.

I think I have a good force for doing that today in the peninsula, but I also rely on PACOM for immediate forces to respond: for example, the air forces stationed in Japan and throughout the PACOM theater; ISR to be responsive; the Marine force and MEF [Marine Expeditionary Force] to be responsive. And we keep a package—"we" being PACOM commander, his force, his subordinate commands, and myself—that we know the readiness of those forces on any given day and any given hour that I need immediately, and we track those, and that is very important to my ability to respond and defend Korea.

Mr. WITTMAN. Thank you, Mr. Chairman.

I yield back.

The CHAIRMAN. Thank you.

General, I have had a request from the recording people, if you would make sure the microphone is right in front of your face, then it seems to work better. Thank you, sir.

Mr. Courtney.

Mr. COURTNEY. Thank you, Mr. Chairman.

And thank you to both witnesses for your leadership and your testimony this morning.

Admiral, on page 5 of your testimony, you pretty much laid out what is sort of the guideposts for the sovereignty claims issues, which we have discussed this morning with the island building, and basically, it says, we encourage all countries to uphold international laws reflected in the Law of the Sea Convention. Should the United States ratify UNCLOS [United Nations Convention on the Law of the Sea], the Law of the Sea treaty?

Admiral HARRIS. Thanks, sir, for the question. Before I answer, I want to just say that I have spent a lot of time talking to proponents and opponents of UNCLOS in the last 3 or 4 months, and I appreciate the time I have spent with those experts, and I understand their arguments. And I understand those arguments for those folks who are opposed to UNCLOS, but I am a proponent of it. And I think, in the 21st century, our moral standing is affected by the fact that we are not a signatory to UNCLOS. I think there are some economic disadvantages as well. We could get into a discussion about the Russian stuff in the Arctic and how they are using UNCLOS to their advantage, and we are unable to because we are not a signatory to it.

So, you know, I will tell the members of this committee and anyone else that for me, personally, my opinion is the United States should accede to UNCLOS.

Mr. COURTNEY. Thank you. And, again, when we discussed this at PACOM earlier, or last fall, that was before the Hague Convention ruled against the United States request to be part of the—just as an observer on the Philippines claim on the Spratly Islands, which Mr. Wittman referred to earlier. I mean, it is kind of unbelievable we are allowing sort of litigation to proceed that the consequences in terms of military strategy and resources of this country in the Asia-Pacific could hinge on the outcome of that claim, and we are completely shut out because of an unforced error. I mean, we have done this to ourselves. And so, you know, thank you for your frankness this morning. Myself and Congressman Don Young are going to introduce a bipartisan resolution in the House, again, citing events in the South China Sea as why we really need to take a fresh look at the Law of the Sea treaty. And, as a nation, we need to move forward and get in the game in terms of, you know, these critical issues, because it is going to determine the course of maritime policy and military policy and budgets for decades to come. So thank you, again, for that input.

Earlier you mentioned the fact that we have a shortage of submarines in the Asia-Pacific. Again, today, we are operating with an attack sub fleet of about 52. Even with the two-a-year build rate that we started in 2011, that is going to continue to drop to, at this point, based on the shipbuilding plan that was submitted last week, to 41. Can you talk about what that will do to future commands in terms of the challenges that you are already facing with a larger fleet size?

Admiral HARRIS. Sure. So PACOM suffers a shortage of submarines today. My requirements are not being met, as are not the requirements of other COCOMs [combatant commands] as well. So we have a submarine force of about 52 attack submarines, and all the COCOMs need them for all their reasons. And when you add up all their requirements, it exceeds the ability of the Navy to provide submarines forward, when you consider a lot of those are in maintenance and a lot of other things.

I worry that we are going to go down to 41, because as we go down to the low 40s, China is going to increase their submarine force, even as they are today. And then Russia, which has the most capable submarine force in the world next to ours, they are moving their latest generation SSBNs, the ballistic missile submarines, to the Pacific. So the *Dolgorukiy*-class SSBNs got there at the end of last year, and that is just the beginning. And then China, meanwhile, has their *Jin,* J–I–N, *Jin*-class SSBNs that they are bringing online, and we are seeing them now.

I feel that I must be able to keep those submarines at risk, and I am able to do so today, but as we go down in numbers, then that becomes a concern to me.

Mr. COURTNEY. All right. Thank you. And we have actually an opportunity on Seapower [Subcommittee] to look at the next block contract, because, frankly, there is a dip in that, and we should do everything we can to avoid that, because that will at least bring the number up somewhat and mitigate, you know, what you just described.

As long as I have 10 seconds left and people are boasting about proximity to Asia-Pacific, if an attack submarine leaves Groton, Connecticut, and goes under the ice, it can actually get there ahead of the folks from Washington State.

And, with that, I yield back, Mr. Chairman.

Mr. LARSEN. Thank God for Connecticut.

The CHAIRMAN. Mr. Franks.

Mr. FRANKS. Well, thank you, Mr. Chairman.

And thank you, General Scaparrotti and Admiral Harris, for being here—all your entourage—for your commitment to protecting us all. We appreciate it. Sometimes you don't get told that enough.

Admiral Harris, I guess I will start out with a really easy question: Are you aware of any collusion between Iran and North Korea with regards to North Korea's intermittent but ongoing nuclear and missile tests?

Admiral HARRIS. Sir, I am not aware of collusion directly. But we know that there is a relationship between North Korea and Iran, but I am not privy to the details of the nuclear collusion, if you will.

Mr. FRANKS. General Scaparrotti, that is your perspective as well?

General SCAPARROTTI. That is mine as well, yes, sir.

Mr. FRANKS. Admiral, your colleague here, General Scaparrotti, called BMD one of USKF's four critical needs and is certainly—that is—but given the unpredictable and belligerent nature of the North Korean regime combined with their steadily increasing ballistic missile technology, how important do you believe this layered missile defense system that we have is in deterring North Korea?

And in light of some of the recent events that I think are pretty serious, can you describe if you think that there are currently enough defense assets in your command to deter or defeat a North Korean ballistic missile attack?

Admiral HARRIS. Well, first, I will talk about the criticality of a layered defense. It is absolutely critical. You know, we have 28,000 American troops on the Korean Peninsula. We have their families. We have several hundred thousand Americans who live and work in South Korea, and the North Korean capability is growing. And they threaten not only our fellow citizens and our allies in Korea; they threaten Japan, they threaten Hawaii, the West Coast in the mainland of the United States, and then potentially the East Coast.

They are on a quest to miniaturize their nuclear weapons and the means to deliver them intercontinentally, and they pose a very real threat to the United States. So I think the layered defense is the only answer to go after the missiles once launched. That means

THAAD—and I am glad we are engaged in consultations with Korea on putting a THAAD battery there—Patriot, Aegis, the whole thing.

Mr. FRANKS. Well, how has the fiscal year 2017 budget request, prioritization of modernization, affected your commands? I mean, do you currently have the assets you need to fight tonight while currently modernizing?

Admiral HARRIS. I am pleased with the fiscal year 2017 budget. I was asked to make comments about it up my chain, and my concerns were addressed, and principally those concerns were in anti-surface weapons and anti-surface ship missiles and in advanced fighter aircraft for the PACOM theater.

Mr. FRANKS. All right. I guess, let me put it this way, and I will address the question to both of you: If there is anything that you feel like that if you had the option that you could increase in terms of your capability, meaning particular area, what would that be?

Admiral HARRIS. In my case, sir, I would ask for more Joint Strike Fighters, more fifth-generation aircraft to go after the A2/AD [anti-access/area denial] threat that we face in the Pacific.

Mr. FRANKS. General Scaparrotti.

General SCAPARROTTI. Sir, I would say, one, high-altitude multi-INT [intelligence] intelligence, surveillance, and reconnaissance assets; and I would go back to the ballistic missile defense assets: for instance, Patriot. It would be ideal to have more Patriot than I have now as opposed to relying on the additional Patriot at crisis. But the fact of the matter is, is that our missile defense forces are stretched. There is great demand around the globe of that for similar kinds of threats; THAAD, for instance, same.

So, you know, if I were to tell you what more could I use and we had the budget to do it, I think those would be my top two right there.

Mr. FRANKS. Well, Mr. Chairman, I am going to do something crazy; I am going to yield back my last 18 seconds.

And thank you, all, very much.

The CHAIRMAN. Chair appreciates that.

Ms. Tsongas.

Ms. TSONGAS. Thank you, Mr. Chairman.

And thank you to our witnesses for being here.

I too just returned from Japan. I was part of a congressional delegation that spent 3 days in Tokyo and 2 days in Okinawa. And I had spent years there—many years ago, I was a high school student there.

And as I hadn't been back in the interim, I really was struck by the tremendous changes in that country but also in the relationship we have developed with Japan. Because at the time I lived there, it was really not too long after World War II, and there was certainly an effort to constrain Japan militarily and, yet, to reassure it about its being protected.

So, as we have moved forward, we are in a very different environment. And I appreciate the rationale for it, as things have really changed in that part of the—in the Asia-Pacific area.

And, Admiral, you referenced the peace and security legislation that Japan just passed that really authorizes it to engage in a more expansive way in regional security efforts. And one of the questions

I had there and posed there was, is money following that? As Japan is sort of—as the ties are being loosened on what it can do and cannot do militarily, is funding following that effort so that they absorb a little more of the financial responsibility for protecting that part of the world?

Admiral HARRIS. Thank you, Congresswoman.

I believe it is, but I don't know that for a fact. I know that the government and the Prime Minister have said that funding will follow, that they are going to fund their aspirations to improve their military and their capability. But I will also add that the primary costs of our U.S. forces in Japan are paid for by Japan.

Ms. TSONGAS. Yes. And what is that amount? I know we were given a figure over there. Do you know off the top of your head?

Admiral HARRIS. No, ma'am, but I will find out before the closed hearing.

Ms. TSONGAS. I would welcome that.

Admiral HARRIS. It is in the hundreds of billions of dollars, but I will find that out and get back to you on that.

[The information was not available at the time of printing.]

Ms. TSONGAS. Thank you for that.

And the other issue that came up too was sort of encouraging jointness between Japan's security forces and our forces as we are seeking ways to work together. And I am wondering how you are thinking that through and encouraging that.

Admiral HARRIS. And encouraging——

Ms. TSONGAS. Jointness, more joint operations between our forces and theirs.

Admiral HARRIS. Yeah. So everything we are doing is joint these days in the U.S. side. And I think the other countries are observing that and learning from that.

So, last fall, we had an SLS, a senior leader seminar, with the Japan Joint Staff, which is their joint headquarters in Tokyo. And we went through some of our war planning and some of our efforts in that arena. So I think Japan recognizes that they need to be more joint within their military than they are, and they are working with us closely to improve their jointness.

So I was honored last week to travel to Japan, and I spoke at the 10th anniversary of the Japan Joint Staff. And I have been associated with Japan, their military, for most of my career, and they are far and away further along in jointness today than they have been. That is not to say that they don't have a ways to go.

And I think that the jointness between their air force and their navy, for example, should be improved, and I think they recognize that. They are moving toward a greater amphibious capability, and that forces a level of cooperation between their ground self-defense force and their maritime self-defense force.

So I am very optimistic about where Japan is going in terms of jointness and their ability to work with us in a joint manner across our services.

Ms. TSONGAS. And that is what I was getting at, was they are working us with as much as they are within the different branches of their services.

Admiral HARRIS. That is right.

Ms. TSONGAS. Thank you.

I too will yield back the balance of my time.

The CHAIRMAN. We are on a roll here.

Mr. Bridenstine.

Mr. BRIDENSTINE. Thank you, Mr. Chairman.

And thank you both for being here. It is an honor to have you before our committee. Certainly, I have spent plenty of time in the Pacific as a Navy pilot myself, now serving in the Oklahoma Air National Guard.

General Scaparrotti, I wanted to ask you or actually share with you one of my big concerns I have heard from one of my constituents. I want to make you aware of a recent Army regulation change regarding dining facility use for rotationally deployed forces under your command. Effective February 15, 2016, the Army declared essential unit messing for rotationally deployed soldiers serving in the Pacific. In other words, all soldiers deployed temporary duty to Korea must use the dining facility, the DFAC.

This policy will literally take money out of soldiers' pockets, hundreds of dollars per month, in two ways: First, the Army will charge for meals at the DFAC through automatic payroll deductions. That is automatic payroll deductions. These deductions will occur whether or not a soldier actually uses the DFAC. And, as you are aware, when you do missions in these areas, those missions happen during breakfast, happen during lunch, and you are not able to use the DFAC. So soldiers will have money deducted, even though they are not using the DFAC.

Second, the Army is also taking away their daily food allowance, known as the government meal rate. I have a constituent in the 10th Combat Aviation Brigade currently at Camp Humphreys. The Army's bureaucratic jiggery-pokery will reduce his paycheck over $700 per month through the automatic DFAC deduction and stopping meal allowances. I want to repeat that: $700 per month. These soldiers are not going to Korea for a week or even a month; they are going for 9 months. And so when you lose $700 a month, that ends up being a good chunk of money.

In contrast, a soldier at Camp Humphreys, under the permanent change of station orders, is apparently exempt from the automatic meal deduction. Aviation units, such as the 10th CAB [Combat Aviation Brigade], don't plan training or missions around the whims of the DFAC, as I have already talked about. That is why the food allowance exists in the first place. That is why it was there.

And I would like to show you some pictures here of what is going on at the DFAC in Korea. There are a couple of pictures. Can we just slide through a few more?

[The slides referred to were not available at the time of printing.]

Mr. BRIDENSTINE. So these soldiers, they are having their money automatically withheld, and then they are being forced to wait in an hour line in order to go through the DFAC. Some of them can't go through the DFAC at all because of missions. When they do go, they are waiting an hour, and that is three times a day. That is 3 hours a day where they are being delayed. Again, this happens three times a day.

I just want to get a commitment from you, General, that you will do something for our soldiers, who are flying, in many cases, high-risk—and these are steady-state missions. This isn't like a surprise. This isn't something that just came up. These are steady-state missions at the DMZ. And, number one, I want to make sure they get their meals. I want to make sure that they are not waiting in line for 3 hours three times a day. And I want to make sure that they are not having their money taken away. Can you commit to me that you will look into this?

General SCAPARROTTI. Absolutely. And I will come back to you personally on it. We have got not only the CAB that you mentioned, but, you know, we have other rotational units, obviously, as a part of our readiness that rotate regularly on 9-month rotations. They are probably affected as well.

[The information was not available at the time of printing.]

Mr. BRIDENSTINE. Okay.

And, Mr. Chairman, before I yield back, I just want to note that I want to introduce legislation to make sure that this is taken care of. Thank you.

I yield back.

The CHAIRMAN. Mr. Takai.

Mr. TAKAI. Thank you, Mr. Chairman.

And thank you, Admiral Harris, General Scaparrotti, for being here.

Admiral Harris, again, regarding the Aegis Ashore facility—or the hope for a facility—North Korea's nuclear test in January underscores the concern that we have, that North Korea may develop the ability to place a bomb on a long-range ballistic missile that could reach the U.S. West Coast. I referred to public comments you made that converting the Aegis missile defense test site in Hawaii into a combat-ready facility is a good idea to help protect the U.S. mainland.

Since we have assets on Kauai, why not use them? How would this permanent land version add to U.S. defense needs? And what would it take to integrate the site into a larger U.S. ballistic missile defense system?

Admiral HARRIS. Thanks, Congressman. Good to see you again.

I believe that we need to do everything we can to defend our Nation, and that is my job in the Pacific. I think the Aegis Ashore facility in Kauai is a national treasure, and we should use it to the best of our ability. And I think one of the ways that we could improve our national ballistic missile defense capability is by converting that to a permanent facility with interceptors. It seems reasonable to me, but it demands further study. It demands a lot of study.

I think, at the end of the day, we will learn that what it will do, it would be able to defend Hawaii, and other systems we have would defend the continental United States. But that is good. I am good with that. And that is what I have recommended, that we begin the study to see if it is feasible and what it would take to do it.

There is not only the technical aspects of the architecture, the ballistic missile defense architecture; there is a political dynamic, as you well know, and the whole piece would increase in footprint in Hawaii and all that. So it is a whole effort that needs to be looked at. But I am advocating it because I think we need to do it.

I noted that after I made that statement, that China objected, just as they have objected to the consultations we have with Korea to put THAAD in Korea. And I find it preposterous that China would insert itself in negotiations between us and our Korean ally on how best to defend our Korean ally and our Americans there, and they would interject themselves in our internal discussions of whether we should improve our ability to defend our own homeland.

Mr. TAKAI. Thank you.

Actually, just a few days ago, China's Foreign Ministry spokeswoman compared the United States military infrastructure in Hawaii to China's land reclamation and strategic placement of missiles on disputed territory in the South China Seas. Can you just tell us your perspective on whether Hawaii should be and could be compared to the disputed territory in the South China Seas?

Admiral HARRIS. Yeah. That statement that the Chinese spokesman made almost doesn't merit comment. I mean, it is ridiculous, and to me, it is indicative of the spokesperson's tone deafness.

Mr. TAKAI. I agree.

In regards to the status of the rebalance, if U.S. defense spending remains limited to the cap set forth in the Budget Control Act of 2011, as amended, the so-called sequester levels, how might this impact the plans for bolstering U.S. force posture and presence in the Asia-Pacific region? And what might be the implications of maintaining deterrence and for operational risk in a potential combat situation?

Admiral HARRIS. As I have testified before, certainly at my confirmation hearing, that I think that if we return to sequester levels for the duration of the law, out to the early 2020s, it will harm our ability dramatically, our ability to defend our Nation. I think all that would be affected. And we are going through that now as we look at downsizing the Army, and should we do that? Where should those forces come from that would be part of the downsizing and everything?

So I have testified before that I think a continued sequester would hurt us significantly in our military readiness, and I stand by that.

Mr. TAKAI. Thank you.

Thank you, Mr. Chairman.

The CHAIRMAN. Thank you.

Mr. Byrne.

Mr. BYRNE. Thank you, Mr. Chairman.

Gentlemen, thank you for being here today.

Admiral Harris, let me ask you some questions about the littoral combat ship [LCS] program. You have stated that the littoral combat ship was a vital capability for you to engage through the PACOM area of operation. You note the LCS was needed to do missions not suited for DDGs, destroyers. How beneficial is having such a capability in your AOR [area of responsibility] to patrol waters not easily navigated by larger platforms?

Admiral HARRIS. Well, thanks for the question, sir. Just by definition, I mean, the littoral combat ship is designed to operate in shallower waters than our destroyers and cruisers. I think in where we are now in phase zero, the LCS is a terrific platform to work with our allies and partners in the region.

I think that there is work, though, that could be done to the LCS to make the "C" more "C," the combat part of littoral combat ship. And I am pleased, through the Senate and the House and the Congress writ large, that we are looking at doing that. So we are going to, quote-unquote, "up-gun" the LCS. And I think that is terrific.

I want our adversaries in the Pacific to think about the LCS the way I thought about the Nanuchkas, Osa's, and Tarantuls of the Soviet Navy back in those days, back during the Cold War. We used to track and be concerned about those little, tiny patrol boats that the Soviets had because they were missile-armed corvettes. And I want the Chinese and the Russians and other adversaries we might have to think about the LCS in that way. And I think we can think of it in that way if we put the right kind of missile on it and up-gun it.

Mr. BYRNE. Of course, that is the plan. As you know, the last, I think, 20 ships in the 52-ship buy would be frigates that would have the up-gun and the more heavier platform. But I guess what I hear you saying is, is that because you have so many of them— and it is a cost-effective way to have so many of them—that it is another way for us to project our strength in a maritime environment, in a shallow-draft environment we find in many of those islands.

Admiral HARRIS. That is correct. I stated when I was the Pacific Fleet commander that I value the LCS. I believe there is a place for LCS in the joint force now that I am the PACOM commander, and I look forward to working with them as they come online.

Mr. BYRNE. You also mentioned how we are able to work with other nations and their navies with littoral combat ship. Could you expand on that some, please?

Admiral HARRIS. Sure. A lot of our friends and partners in the region have small navies. And they want to learn from us or they want to learn from somebody, and I would rather they learn from us than other potential partners. And their navies are small. And when a cruiser comes in there or even a DDG for that matter, it can overwhelm them. And so an LCS is the right platform to do that.

It is also the right platform to train in areas of shallower depths, just by definitions, as I talked about, and the cruisers are smaller so that footprint is smaller. And, for that reason, I think in a partnership environment way, the LCS is, again, an ideal platform.

Mr. BYRNE. Let me ask you about another vessel. It is called the joint high-speed vessel [JHSV]. They just renamed it the EPF [expeditionary fast transport]. And I understand that those vessels are getting some pretty good use in PACOM. This is a well-built ship with ability to add a lot of additional capabilities. What do you see as the future of the joint high-speed vessel, the EPF, in your AOR?

Admiral HARRIS. I think it has great potential for some of the mission sets that I have to be concerned about, more so the Pacific Fleet commander would worry about it. But the joint high-speed vessel has a great ability to move a lot of things quickly. And by "a lot of things," I mean, troops and their equipment. And the Army is using a version of that now in the western Pacific.

So I am looking forward to the JHSV EPF coming online in greater numbers. I think that you could put an expedition or a field hospital, for example, on a JHSV and turn it into a hospital ship. We explored that in the last few months in my time as Pacific Fleet commander during Pacific Partnership. That is an exciting new capability that I think we should take a hard look at.

Mr. BYRNE. Well, thank you for your service, gentlemen, both of you.

And I yield back.

The CHAIRMAN. Mr. Johnson.

Mr. JOHNSON. Thank you, Mr. Chairman.

And thank you, gentlemen, for your service.

The U.S. PAC [Pacific] Command has given authorization in the fiscal year 2016 NDAA's South China Sea initiative to build our maritime security in the region and improve the domain awareness of our partners in the region. In your opinion, does this authority need to be expanded, and if so, what changes would you like to see made?

Admiral HARRIS. Sir, that is the maritime security initiative. I am pleased with where we are with it now. I think we will get about $50 million this year for that. My team is working with OSD [Office of the Secretary of Defense] on that to figure out the best ways to improve the maritime domain awareness of some of the countries in the region, and I am satisfied with where we are with that this year.

Mr. JOHNSON. Thank you.

General. Anything you would add, General?

General SCAPARROTTI. No, sir. Thank you.

Mr. JOHNSON. All right. Thank you.

Admiral, you mentioned in your testimony PAC Command's need for enduring cyber capability in the theater. Cyber warfare is undoubtedly a growing aspect of modern warfare and something we must strive to be ahead of as much as possible. Would making USCYBERCOM [U.S. Cyber Command] a combatant command like CENTCOM [Central Command] help funnel focus and funding to a vitally important aspect of this new theater of warfare?

Admiral HARRIS. In my opinion, sir, CYBERCOM should be an independent combatant command.

Mr. JOHNSON. Would you pull that mike closer.

Admiral HARRIS. Yeah. In my opinion, sir, CYBERCOM should be an independent combatant command on the level of PACOM or CENTCOM, as you say. Currently, it is a sub-unified command under USSTRATCOM [U.S. Strategic Command].

Mr. JOHNSON. Do you have any thoughts on how Congress can be effective in helping bring that about?

Admiral HARRIS. No, sir. I think it is being addressed adequately within DOD [Department of Defense], and ultimately, the Chairman will make his best military advice known to both the President and the Secretary and a decision will be rendered. And I think that is appropriate in this case at this time.

Mr. JOHNSON. Thank you.

General, anything to add?

General SCAPARROTTI. No, sir. I agree with Admiral Harris. I know it is under discussion now. And I think the DOD, as he said, is considering that, and it will be handled in a normal process.

Mr. JOHNSON. Thank you.

Admiral, considering Vietnam's claims in the Spratly and Paracel Islands and rising patriotism in Vietnam, and animosity towards China resulting from the 2014 oil rig standoff, and Hanoi becoming the eighth largest arms importer from 2011 to 2015, a maritime dispute between China and Vietnam in the South China Sea has perhaps the greatest possibility for becoming a flash point in the region.

However, in recent public discussions on the issue of the South China Sea, it has been surprising to understand the dearth of information on our engagement with Vietnam. Most of the focus has been instead on our defense treaty with the Philippines and their arbitration case. Moving forward, do you see a place for increased bilateral dialogue between the U.S. and Vietnam, and if so, what developments would you like to see?

Admiral HARRIS. So I have made Vietnam and India focuses— foci—focuses, I guess, of effort for PACOM. I think there are great opportunities in both countries for us to move forward in our relationship and partnerships in the region. So I am excited by our opportunities in Vietnam just for the reasons you mentioned. You know, they are a growing nation. They have a like view with us of China and our concerns in the South China Sea. And they are becoming a player on the world stage, and they are certainly a player in ASEAN [Association of Southeast Asian Nations].

So I look forward to continuing our relationship with Vietnam. I appreciate the fact we are able to increase our trade with Vietnam, including in the defense arena. I went to Vietnam when I was a Pacific Fleet commander, and I look forward to having the opportunity to go there as a Pacific Command commander.

Mr. JOHNSON. All right. Thank you.

Anything to add, General?

General SCAPARROTTI. No, thank you. Thank you, sir.

Mr. JOHNSON. Thank you.

I yield back, Mr. Chairman.

The CHAIRMAN. Ms. McSally.

Ms. MCSALLY. Thank you, Mr. Chairman.

Thank you, gentlemen.

General Scaparrotti, you said earlier that should we have to be involved—God forbid—in military conflict on the peninsula, it would be more akin to Korea or World War II: complex, high casualty. Are you concerned at all—we have heard, you know, the service chiefs come before us in the last year, sequestration, the impact, and us being in 15 years of a counterinsurgency mindset has had a real impact on the readiness of units. The squadron I commanded was ready to head over there on 24 hours' notice, but a lot of the readiness has really been degraded across the joint force that are on a TPFDD [time-phased force and deployment data] ready to go for supporting that kind of contingency. Are you concerned at all about the real readiness levels of being able to respond quickly?

General SCAPARROTTI. Yes, ma'am. Thank you. Yes, I am. As you know, all of our services are really coming out of a bathtub in readiness, and it has been improving because of the increased funding. And we appreciate that support, but it is going to be some time before our forces are at a point where all of the units have now been through training that prepares them really for a complex environment, high-intensity conflict.

I can speak specifically of the Army. It takes time for us to get units through those complex rotations at our national training centers. We have got younger generations who haven't combined fires, for instance, et cetera, fire and maneuver in large formations. Those are things that an individual, small unit, and larger unit training that is complex.

So I am concerned about it. I know that all the services are focused on this, and we, on the peninsula, are as well. So, when we do our exercises and we bring units in, that is the kind of training at each level that we are focused on.

Ms. MCSALLY. Great. I am interested in following up a little bit more in the classified session as well as far as the risks we are at right now.

General SCAPARROTTI. Thank you.

Ms. MCSALLY. I think I also heard you say in the shortage of munitions that you mentioned that the potential cluster munition ban and the impact that that would have on your ability to do your job. I just want to make sure I understood that.

Neither the U.S. nor South Korea are signatories to the cluster munition ban, so can you just clarify what you meant? And if we were to become a signatory and those would be banned, what impact would that have on munition?

General SCAPARROTTI. That is correct, neither signatories. However, the U.S. has a policy that in 2019, in January of 2019, we would essentially comply with the Oslo treaty through policy.

Ms. MCSALLY. So what impact would that have?

General SCAPARROTTI. The impact for me would be significant because the majority of my munitions are cluster munitions that are affected by that policy. And, of course, then what I am concerned about and the reason I am bringing it up now is we need to begin to replace those munitions so that I have the proper stockage for the first 30 days on site.

Cluster munitions in and of themselves provide an effect that in this fight is very important, is very difficult to replicate with unitary rounds. So we need to get to a cluster munition. We need to keep this cluster munition until such time that we are able to produce a replacement that meets the less than 1 percent dud rate and we can produce it in numbers to meet my need.

Ms. MCSALLY. But just to clarify, it would be best for the military mission that you have for that ban to not go into effect?

General SCAPARROTTI. That is correct. That is what I mean by we need to keep what we have and be able to use it until we can replace it properly.

Ms. MCSALLY. Thank you.

Admiral Harris, I want to talk a little bit about the ISIS [Islamic State in Iraq and Syria] threat and how you are seeing that in the whole theater. I am on Homeland Security as well. You know, looking at the foreign fighter flow, we know there is at least a couple thousand coming from your theater—China, Indonesia, some from Australia—that we are aware of; also, about a half a dozen affiliates that have allegiance to ISIS; and obviously, the Jakarta bombing that ISIS claimed in January.

Can you just talk about the trends you are seeing? And is there any concern with us or our allies in the direction this is going?

Admiral HARRIS. Yes, ma'am. It is a significant concern of mine, the numbers of fighters that are leaving PACOM countries and going to the fight. Of greater concern are those, however, that are returning because not only are they even more radicalized; now they are militarized, weaponized, and so that is a concern.

I am concerned by some of the trends I am seeing in the region. In one of the countries, recently, there was a Pew survey where over 50 percent of the respondents said it was okay to execute a Muslim who converted to some other religion; 30 percent of the respondents in that country said it was okay to use violence in the name of Islam. That sounds like something coming right out of the pages of the ISIS handbook. So I worry about that quite a bit.

I made the comment in the past that there are more Muslims in the PACOM region than in Central Command.

Ms. MCSALLY. Exactly.

Admiral HARRIS. And so Islamic extremism is an area of concern, as I mentioned in my opening statement, and we look at that very closely. And fortunately, Special Operations Command Pacific, SOCPAC, is there, and Admiral Kilrain is charged with monitoring that and having an effect on that.

Ms. MCSALLY. Great. Thanks. My time is expired. Thanks.

The CHAIRMAN. Mr. Langevin.

Mr. LANGEVIN. Thank you, Mr. Chairman.

Admiral Harris and General Scaparrotti, thank you very much for your testimony today and your service to our Nation.

For years now, we have underinvested in our EW [electronic warfare] capabilities, where our adversaries have actually invested heavily in those areas. Now, some of this you may not be able to go into an open session, but to the degree that you can, where are we held risk because of that underinvestment as we are shifting to the Asia-Pacific region? And how overmatched are we? And what areas do we further need to invest? And where are our adversaries' capabilities strongest? What keeps you awake at night should conflict ever break out and we need to confront this?

Admiral HARRIS. Thanks, sir.

In trying to dance on the unclassified side of this question, I will say that I am concerned about principally in the EW environment with Russia and China. They are our peer competitors in this. I think we are investing now more than we have been in electronic warfare, and our new concept electronic warfare maneuver, I think, is gaining a foothold in the Navy and in the joint force.

So I am pleased with where we are moving along, though I think that we need to invest more in it, not only in terms of fiscal resources but also in terms of tactical development.

Mr. LANGEVIN. General, do you want to add anything?

General SCAPARROTTI. Yeah, I would agree. I think that our investment in that has been periodic, and as a result, we have seen the need, started to respond to it, and then probably dropped off over time, I think, specifically over the last 10 years. And we are now beginning to invest in that in terms of our people, our skills, and our assets, and I think we need to continue that.

Mr. LANGEVIN. Admiral Harris, in your testimony, you highlighted that the world's 300 foreign submarines, 200 are located in the Indo-Asia-Pacific region, and 150 of those belong to China, North Korea, and Russia. How is the United States keeping pace with this growing force in the region, and what investments need to be made to enhance our undersea and antisubmarine warfare capabilities as well as to our anti-access and area denial strategies?

Admiral HARRIS. So one of the biggest asymmetric advantages that the United States enjoys over any peer competitor or other competitor in the world is our undersea warfare capability. The submarine gives us an advantage over any other adversary we might face. Unfortunately, those adversaries recognize that, and they are improving and increasing their own antisubmarine warfare and undersea warfare capabilities.

Clearly, while our submarines are far and away better, in my opinion, today, quantity has a quality all its own, and the numbers of Russian and Chinese submarines, particularly Chinese submarines, are a matter of concern. I think the Russian submarine force never took a hiatus at the end of the Cold War, and we are seeing some very impressive platforms come out of Russia, including the Dolgorukiy, as I mentioned earlier, the SSBN.

So I think that we must continue to invest in our undersea warfare capabilities, not only in terms of numbers of submarines but in improving the submarines that we have. I think the *Virginia* Payload Module, for example, is fantastic. We can't get enough of them and the capabilities that it brings to the fight.

Mr. LANGEVIN. Good. Thank you.

I would like to shift, if I could, to cyber. And I have a pretty good understanding of our cyber capabilities. But, again, as we are shifting to the Asia-Pacific and we are going to be partnering more closely with our allies in the region, where is your level of confidence in their cyber capabilities should we need to partner with them and should conflict break out?

I know the challenges that we face in securing our own systems, but to the degree that we are going to be dependent on our allies in the region and their cyber capabilities, which may be not as robust as what ours are.

Admiral HARRIS. Thank you, sir. I will defer to General Scaparrotti for the specifics of your question with regard to Korea. He has some ideas on that.

But, in general, I am concerned about it. As we work on this with our allies, friends, and partners, we are as strong as only the weakest link in the chain, and cyber could be that weak link. And so their vulnerability to intrusion and exploitation is a matter of concern to me.

General SCAPARROTTI. Sir, I would echo Admiral Harris' point with respect to Korea as well. We have a good working relationship in terms of our two joint cyber centers and our cyber domain work overall, but it is initial. It is new, and it is developing, and it needs to develop rapidly, because we have a threat. North Korea is active every day. And so my concern is that we act with enough focus and we act fast enough and with enough assets.

The second thing I would say, when you are into that domain, each country has their own concerns about protection of information and capabilities, and so it is an area that is very difficult to work in a collaborative way that you need to at times as well. And that is something that we have got and other nations have to work their way through in order to really close the gaps that we have got to close in our systems.

Mr. LANGEVIN. Thank you.

Thank you, Mr. Chairman.

The CHAIRMAN. Thank you.

Ms. Gabbard.

Ms. GABBARD. Thank you, Mr. Chairman.

Gentlemen, welcome. Aloha. I am not going to harp on this, but I will mention it quickly. I know it has been talked earlier about the Aegis Ashore on Kauai and just the paramount importance of protecting Hawaii and the United States from North Korea's threat.

But, Admiral Harris, I would like to talk to you a little bit about India. I know you have a trip very soon to go and visit India. Two things: there is a potential sale of eight F–16s to Pakistan that I and other Members of Congress have expressed very serious concerns about, given the fact that Pakistan has long harbored and given safe haven to various terrorist groups that continue to launch destabilizing attacks within India as well as Afghanistan; the recent release of Hafiz Saeed, one of the masterminds of the 2008 Mumbai terrorist attack, where six U.S. citizens were killed, even at the protests of the United States.

There are a number of other concerns that we have. But, in particular, I am wondering if you can talk about how, as you and others have spoken of the importance of this opportunity to strengthen our relationship with India as we head into a strong partnership into the future and the benefits that that brings us, what impact could this sale of F–16s have on our relationship with India and the work that you and others are doing to strengthen that?

Admiral HARRIS. That is a great question and timely too, ma'am, because I go to India on Monday to keynote the Raisina Dialogue event in New Delhi.

I view India as our great strategic opportunity in PACOM, and we need to do as much as we can with India in a mil-to-mil sense and in every other sense. We have a terrific ambassador there in Richard Verma, who is looking aggressively at ways to improve our relationships with India across the board. And I am excited by that.

With regard to the sale of F–16s to Pakistan, while I don't have a professional opinion on that sale itself, certainly it will affect some aspect of our relationship with India. I know that I will be asked about it when I go to India, and I hope to be able to tell them that that sale is just one aspect of many military sales we make across the world, and that we view our relationship with India very importantly. And I hope that we can work through this sale and their perception of it to continue to improve our relationship with India.

Ms. GABBARD. Yeah, thank you. I think this is something that they will definitely be bringing up with you at that dialogue, in particular because of the recent attack at their air force base and the terrorist organization behind that being from Pakistan.

What do you see here really as the next critical step towards strengthening that U.S.-India partnership?

Admiral HARRIS. So we are moving out aggressively in the technical field with the DTTI [Defense Technology and Trade Initiative] initiative that Under Secretary Kendall is pushing. And I think that is excellent. There are some what we call foundational agreements that have to be executed with partner nations in order to move, quote-unquote, to the next level. And we are working with India on the signing of those foundational agreements.

One of those is the LSA, Logistics Support Agreement, which allows us to do acquisition cross-servicing, for example. Another one is called the CISMOA [Communications and Information Security Memorandum of Agreement], and it involves communications security so that we can be assured that India will protect our communications as we would protect theirs. And so these are foundation agreements that we enact with every country we work with.

We have not gotten to the point of signing them with India, but I think we are close. We are closer now than we ever have been. And I am encouraged by what I am hearing from my colleagues in India, and I look forward to having that discussion with them when I go there next week.

Ms. GABBARD. Great.

Thank you, Admiral Harris. I appreciate the leadership that you have taken, in particular on strengthening this relationship and recognizing the importance of it in our overall strategy within the Asia-Pacific. Thank you.

The CHAIRMAN. Mr. O'Rourke.

Mr. O'ROURKE. Thank you, Mr. Chairman.

Admiral, I would like to ask you to discuss and provide some guidance for me and others on how to approach the issue of cost sharing for our obligations and the benefits that we provide in the Pacific.

The easy way for me to look at it when it comes to Europe is through the 27 other NATO members who have a target of spending at least 2 percent of GDP on defense, even though only 4 of them today are doing that. But it is something that I can ask of our allies who enjoy the benefit of the U.S. disproportionate presence there and defense capacity.

How should I look at that when it comes to Asia and the Pacific?

Admiral HARRIS. A great question, sir. And I think that the NATO model, as I mentioned before, doesn't work for the Pacific. So you have to look at each of our treaty allies individually and look at those—that subset of treaty allies where we have major concentrations of U.S. forces. And who is the greater beneficiary of that, or who are the beneficiaries of that?

Certainly, part of the beneficiary of us having a large carrier strike group bring expeditionary force presence in Japan is us. We are there for us and the values that we hold dear and what is important to the United States. Certainly, it is a benefit to Japan. And so our obligation to Japan under our treaty is to defend them and their obligation to us under that same treaty is to provide us a place from which we can defend them. So that is simplistic, but that sort of gets at that issue.

So they provide us an enormous host nation funding level—which I promised I would get to you in the closed session—to foot the bill, if you will, for U.S. forces that are based in Japan. And that model extends to Australia, for example. We are undergoing host nation funding discussions with Australia now as we move a sizable Marine and Air Force presence to Darwin and Tindal. And the level of that funding and how much it should be is a subject of negotiation. We certainly get a benefit from operating out of Australia, as do the Australians.

Singapore is another case, a very important case. Singapore is not a treaty ally, but it is certainly an important strategic partner to us. And they allow us to put our littoral combat ships, to rotationally deploy them out of their nation, and they have agreed to allow us to operate rotationally P–3s and P–8 surveillance and reconnaissance aircraft. And we get that benefit from operating out of Singapore because of our interests in the South China Sea, Strait of Malacca, and the eastern Indian Ocean.

Mr. O'ROURKE. Yeah. All of that makes sense, and I think that same logic could extend to our presence in Europe, and yet there we have a very defined commitment from our allies there. As you outline some of the challenges that we face, a rising China, a resurgent Russia, just to name two, and some of the investments that you are going to ask or the Department of Defense and the administration will ask the taxpayer to make, all of which I think are sound, I think it is also an appropriate time to think about what our allies and other beneficiaries in the Asia-Pacific region should expect to contribute. And we, the taxpayer, the Representatives should have a clear understanding of that.

And I don't know if, General Scaparrotti, if you want to talk about Korea as an example with the THAAD batteries and Patriot missile battery deployments there, use that as an example. What part of that cost is shared by—understand the benefit to us of having our service members and those defenses there. What does Korea share in that in terms of cost?

General SCAPARROTTI. I would just say that this is a unique alliance with the U.S.-ROK Alliance, and it has started and has grown since the Korean War. And in this case, we have got a treaty partner and a partner that spends 2.5 percent pretty routinely each year in their defense. And they spend portions of their defense money to meet commitments that we have agreed upon mutually that they need to develop in order to strengthen the alliance. And in the closed session, we can talk specifically about that.

Secondly, through negotiations, they also—called a special measures agreement—they annually pay a certain percentage of the cost of U.S. forces to be stationed in Korea and assist in their defense. So I think it is a good construct. They are great partners in this respect. And they have been true to the—they have the same funding challenges that we have, but they have been true to meeting their commitments in that respect.

Mr. O'ROURKE. Thank you very much.

Thank you, Mr. Chairman.

The CHAIRMAN. Ms. Duckworth.

Ms. DUCKWORTH. Thank you, Mr. Chairman.

Admiral Harris, it is good to see you here again.

My question is actually for General Scaparrotti. It has to do with the Army's ARI [Aviation Restructure Initiative] and how that is going to affect the combat aviation brigades in Korea. In Korea, the Army will be relying on rotational forces if this ARI is complete, as opposed to a CAB that is stationed there.

The National Commission on the Future of the Army recommended keeping a CAB permanently assigned to the peninsula, because short-term rotations—and I am quoting—"short-term rotations will not permit aviation units the time needed to properly mitigate risks posed by the threat situation in Korea, and, specifically, rotating units will not have time to master the geographic and environmental conditions well enough to operate effectively and safely in the region."

Obviously, Korea is a country with numerous terrain and extreme weather conditions. Our aviation crews will have to be able to operate in all sorts of environments, and they are, but a permanently assigned unit there will be better able to handle and maintain proficiency.

Permanently stationing a CAB in Korea would come with a significant upfront price tag as well as enduring costs. So, despite the operational concerns, the fiscal reality is that it just might not be realistic. Your written testimony lays out an array of complex threats that we face on the peninsula. So I think that, despite the cost, it is worth discussing.

As a commander, which force structure—a rotational force or a permanently stationed combat aviation brigade—do you feel best enables you to meet the threats and operational needs in the peninsula?

General SCAPARROTTI. Thank you for the question.

We have a permanently stationed combat aviation brigade there now, and there is discussion about perhaps going to a rotational one. I completely agree with the commission in terms of this is an environment that is difficult to fly in, mountainous, weather. It is an environment that they also have to fly in close proximity to an adversary that will shoot at them.

Ms. DUCKWORTH. Right.

General SCAPARROTTI. And, third, we have mission sets there that are joint in nature. We do a lot of work with our air and our naval forces off the coast. And as a result of that, it is very difficult to get pilots to that level of proficiency, come into the peninsula, and, in a 9-month rotation, be able to sustain that, because some of that simply has to be done on the peninsula after they arrive.

And because of that, I have said that I do not agree with a rotational force in Korea. I think it will produce a less-ready force, and also, it will be more dangerous for our crews.

Ms. DUCKWORTH. Thank you.

Do you think politically—well, for our allied militaries, do you think a rotational force will signal to the ROK a decrease in U.S. commitment to the region's defenses? Is there a perception on their side that switching to rotational force would give them?

General SCAPARROTTI. Well, I think the key to this is what force you do rotate and their readiness when they arrive. For instance, I agree with the forces that we rotate today. We are now rotating an armored brigade, for instance, and the ROKs are fully in support of this. But our commitment is that we deliver one that is combat-ready, fully manned, and also has been trained culturally for that environment. That is something that we have to do.

And I think as long as—I know for the Republic of Korea—as long as we meet that commitment, they will be supportive of using a rotational force. Now, I think there is a certain base that we have there that is permanent, and we have got to maintain that. You couldn't go to a larger percentage of that rotational force. I personally wouldn't be in support of that. But for the specific needs that we have today that we have asked for a rotational force, it has been productive.

Ms. DUCKWORTH. Okay. Great. Thank you.

I want to transfer onto whether or not the Korean wartime operational control transfer is ever going to really happen. You know, we have pushed this off. Do you think they will ever be ready? Are there conditions that need to be in place, metrics that we are looking for?

General SCAPARROTTI. First, yes, they will be ready. They are a modern force, and they are working hard to, one, improve their capabilities but also build the capabilities they need. In the OPCON [operational control] transition plan that was—again, another step was taken that in October between the two Secretaries, we have laid out in detail the capabilities that they have to meet, and we are now working on the next layer of that that provides the timelines on each of those capabilities.

Generally, we have agreed on those in the past. We are confirming those this year, and they are already working on most of those as well. So, yes, I think there will be an OPCON transition. I, too, believe that it should be conditional, not time based. And in the closed session, I can talk in a little more detail on the commitments that we have mutually made to ensure that we can bring that about.

Ms. DUCKWORTH. Thank you. I look forward to that classified briefing.

The CHAIRMAN. Admiral, Mr. O'Rourke made a passing reference to Russia. We see increasing Russia in Europe, in the Middle East. Are you seeing that in the behavior of their ships and planes and so forth?

Admiral HARRIS. I am, Mr. Chairman. We are seeing in the Pacific, as I mentioned before, their new *Dolgorukiy*-class SSBN. I remind folks that there are 3,000 miles of Russian coastline that is in my area of responsibility, including six major strategic bases from which they deploy their submarines, their ships, and their long-range bomber aircraft.

We are seeing long-range bomber aircraft patrols increasing in East Asia. They circumvented Japan just recently. And their ship task forces are operating in the region as well.

The CHAIRMAN. We often don't think of Russia in your theater, but as you just described it, they have a big presence there.

Admiral HARRIS. Yes, sir. I think of them often.

The CHAIRMAN. I appreciate the fact that you do.

I recently had someone say that they were meeting with a Chinese official who said explicitly: You are the past; we are the future.

I think many of us had not expected the degree of aggression, provocation just within the past few years that we see from China. Do you believe that that is their attitude, and do you have a reason why we are seeing it seemingly sped up, certainly in their activities in the South China Sea?

Admiral HARRIS. Mr. Chairman, I do believe that that is their attitude. As I testified yesterday, I think they are on—they have a goal of certainly regional hegemony, and they would like to see the United States out of what they consider their affairs.

But I think that their provocations are causing the other countries in the region to look hard at their relationships with China, and they are turning to the United States as their security partner of choice. And you have to ask yourself why these countries, who were formally leaders in the Non-Aligned Movement, for example, are turning away from China and turning toward the United States, not only giving us access to their bases for our ability to operate but increasingly in terms of trade and military interoperability.

So I think that the statement from China that, quote, "We are the future, and you are the past," unquote, I think that is another indication of the tone deafness of the spokesman who made that comment.

The CHAIRMAN. Fair point. The key for us then is to be a reliable, credible partner for these nations who are turning to us, and that gets back to the responsibilities of this committee, in part.

Thank you both for being here and testifying. I think, if it is okay with you all's schedule, what I would like to do is just within about 5 minutes or so reconvene upstairs in our SCIF, 2337, and continue on a classified or have a classified discussion.

But, for now, this hearing stands adjourned.

[Whereupon, at 12:02 p.m., the committee proceeded to classified session.]

APPENDIX

FEBRUARY 24, 2016

PREPARED STATEMENTS SUBMITTED FOR THE RECORD

FEBRUARY 24, 2016

**Ranking Member Adam Smith Statement on Asia-Pacific Hearing
February 24, 2016**

I would like to welcome Admiral Harris and General Scapparotti and to thank them for appearing before the committee today.

The Indo-Asia-Pacific region is vital to our national interests, and our government has consistently relied on the U.S. military to support a variety of diplomatic, economic, and developmental objectives in the region. The United States will continue to promote growth and prosperity through its committed presence in the region.

It is appropriate that we assess the methods and capabilities of other countries in the Indo-Asia-Pacific region and the challenges that those methods and capabilities may present. However, our efforts to guard against concerning methods and capabilities should not presume that conflict in the region is inevitable. Rather, they should be geared toward ensuring good faith observance and preservation of international order. That said, recent events have demonstrated that there are significant difficulties in the region. These factors must be thoughtfully considered as we seek to maintain a significant U.S. military capability advantage throughout the Indo-Asia-Pacific region.

Unfortunately, North Korea continues to pose a threat to the international community. It is especially troubling that the North Korean regime resorts to bellicosity, brinksmanship, and open provocation to further its objectives. North Korea's efforts to test nuclear and missile capabilities have flagrantly underscored its defiance of the international call for a nuclear-free Korean peninsula. They may also signal willingness on the part of the regime to employ asymmetric or hybrid warfare methods to reinforce its survivability and to exert undue influence. Clearly, we must coordinate closely with our regional allies to adapt, as necessary, to deter, contain and marginalize the dangerous, and often unpredictable, North Korean regime. Reinforcing our missile defense posture on the peninsula against the North Korean threat in coordination with South Korea is one step in the right direction. It would also help to promote stability, if China would coordinate its efforts to peacefully de-nuclearize the Korean peninsula with those of the United States and South Korea.

It would also benefit regional stability, if China would refrain from pressing its claims in the South China Sea in a militaristic fashion and abide by internationally accepted norms applicable to the global commons. Although largely symbolic, evidence of Chinese military activity on Woody Island in the Paracel island chain is a step in the wrong direction. Rather than contribute to a peaceful and equitable resolution to the many disputed claims in the South China Sea, China's actions have shown that it too may be resorting to gray zone tactics short of open conflict to achieve its foreign policy goals.

These developments emphasize the need for persistent U.S. engagement in the region. As the Administration's rebalancing efforts gain momentum, the United States should continue to bolster collective security; help to peaceably address concerns and mitigate disputes; reinforce international laws, standards, and norms; promote shared interests and objectives; facilitate productive multi-lateral exchanges; encourage democratization efforts; and reinforce ties with our many allies and partners.

As our involvement in the vitally important Indo-Asia-Pacific region continues to develop, I will work to help optimize efforts for imparting a positive and lasting effect.

STATEMENT OF
ADMIRAL HARRY B. HARRIS JR., U.S. NAVY
COMMANDER, U.S. PACIFIC COMMAND
BEFORE THE HOUSE ARMED SERVICES COMMITTEE
ON U.S. PACIFIC COMMAND POSTURE
24 FEB 2016

Chairman Thornberry, Congressman Smith, and distinguished members of the committee, thank you for the opportunity to appear before you today. This is my first posture assessment since taking command of U.S. Pacific Command (USPACOM) in May 2015. Over the past 9 months, I've had the extraordinary privilege to lead 378,000 Soldiers, Sailors, Airmen, Marines, Coast Guardsmen, and civilians selflessly serving our nation. These dedicated men and women and their families are doing an amazing job, and I'm proud to serve alongside them.

USPACOM protects and defends, in concert with other U.S. Government agencies, the territory of the U.S., its people, and its interests. With allies and partners, USPACOM enhances stability in the Indo-Asia-Pacific region by promoting security cooperation, encouraging peaceful development, responding to contingencies, deterring aggression, and, when necessary, fighting to win. This approach is based on military preparedness, partnership, and presence.

The strategic importance of the Indo-Asia-Pacific region cannot be overstated. Recognition of clear military, economic, and demographic trends inspired President Obama to undertake a "Rebalance" strategy in 2011. The Rebalance, a strategic whole of government effort, guides and reinforces our military efforts, integrating with diplomatic, political, and economic initiatives.

In August of 2015, Secretary of Defense Carter described four elements of the military component of the Asia-Pacific Rebalance:

1) investing in future capabilities relevant to the challenges in the Asia-Pacific;
2) fielding the right numbers of existing capabilities to the Asia-Pacific;
3) adapting our regional force posture; and
4) reinforcing alliances and partnerships.

Despite other pressing challenges around the world, and because of the legislative and budgetary support of Congress, we achieved momentum in each element above. I believe we must continue, and even increase, this momentum, as the strategic imperative behind the Rebalance remains valid.

What follows is my assessment of the Indo-Asia-Pacific and USPACOM's part of the Rebalance. I will describe the security challenges and highlight regional opportunities with strategic value. I will discuss the value of U.S. strategic force posture and forward presence to the Rebalance - how it improves our readiness to fight tonight, enhances our ability to reassure allies and partners, and maintain stability. I will then explain how USPACOM strengthens our alliances and builds critical regional partnerships that deliver strategic benefit while enhancing U.S. readiness to protect and defend U.S. interests. Finally, I will highlight critical needs and seek your support for budgetary and legislative actions in the coming weeks and months.

Security Environment

The Indo-Asia-Pacific has been a largely peaceful region for over 70 years, in large part, because of the system of rules and norms established and underpinned by robust U.S. presence and anchored by a series of treaty alliances and bilateral relationships with countries in the region. Regional nations, including and perhaps especially China, have benefited because of the security architecture provided by the U.S. and our allies. The Indo-Asia-Pacific is critically important to U.S. commerce, diplomacy, and security. Estimates predict up to 70 percent of the world's population will reside in the region by the middle of this century. Within the region are the world's two largest economies after the U.S. (China and Japan), and five of the smallest economies. The region contains the world's most populous nation (China), largest democracy (India), largest Muslim-majority state (Indonesia), and smallest republic (Nauru). It contains seven of the ten largest standing militaries in the world, five nuclear nations, and five of the U.S.' seven mutual defense treaty alliances.

The region's environment, history, cultural and political diversity, and robust military capabilities present dynamic strategic challenges. Self-interested actors challenge the existing international rules-based order that helped underwrite peace and prosperity in the region for over 70 years. North Korea continues its provocative, coercive behavior and weapons development. Chinese coercion, artificial island construction, and militarization in the South China Sea threaten the most fundamental aspect of global prosperity - freedom of navigation. Other challenges include the movement and facilitation of violent extremists to and from the Middle East, transnational criminal activity (including human trafficking and illicit drugs), and an increasingly revanchist and assertive Russia. USPACOM enhances U.S. force posture, presence, and resiliency in the region, modernizing U.S. force capability to ensure forces are ready to fight and win any contingency. USPACOM is working with allies and partners on a bilateral - and increasingly multilateral - basis to address these challenges. Together, we enhance capability and capacity to respond to the range of threats endemic to the region. We are stronger together.

Overview

A number of challenges has emerged over the past year that place stability and security at risk. In July 2015, China largely completed land reclamation at seven sites in the South China Sea and is finishing runways, infrastructure, and systems to militarize what are, in effect, man-made bases, significantly raising regional tensions. China views the South China Sea as a strategic frontline in their quest to dominate East Asia out to the Second Island Chain. I view their thinking as approaching a new "Great Game." Last month, North Korea conducted its fourth nuclear test in ten years and last August, raised tensions with a land-mine attack in the Demilitarized Zone (DMZ). Russia continues modernizing its military forces, homeporting its newest Dolgurukiy-class ballistic missile submarine in Petropavlovsk, and revitalizing its ability to execute long range strategic patrols, highlighted by last July's deployment of Tu-95 Bear bombers near Alaska and California, and last month's bomber flights around Japan. Terrorist attacks in Bangladesh and Indonesia underscore the fact that violent Islamic extremism is a global problem.

While these events threaten the region's peace and prosperity, there was positive progress as well. Last September, Japan passed its Peace and Security Legislation which authorizes collective self-defense in limited circumstances. The Philippines remained committed to solving its maritime dispute with China peacefully through arbitration under the Law of the Sea Convention. The Philippine Supreme Court upheld the Philippine's domestic approval of the Enhanced Defense Cooperation Agreement (EDCA), which will provide significant partnership and access benefits. India underscored its "Act East" policy by crafting a Joint Strategic Vision of the Asia-Pacific and Indian Ocean Region with the U.S. and is progressing toward signing essential foundational agreements that will enable deeper ties, improve interoperability, and increase cooperation. Singapore has increased routine access to U.S. military assets such as

Littoral Combat Ships and P-3/P-8 aircraft. Trilateral cooperation among allies is increasing and multilateral forums such as the Association of South East Nations (ASEAN) are focusing on shared security challenges in the region. These events demonstrate that Indo-Asia-Pacific countries are increasingly viewing the U.S. as their security partner of choice. That said, significant challenges remain.

Key Challenges

North Korea: Though North Korea is not yet an existential threat to the U.S., it remains the most dangerous and unpredictable actor in the Indo-Asia-Pacific. Kim Jung Un regularly conducts provocative and escalatory actions. Just last month, North Korea conducted an underground nuclear test, the fourth since 2006, which violated its obligations and commitments under international law, including several UN Security Council Resolutions. Additionally, this month, North Korea conducted a ballistic missile test under the guise of launching a satellite. These tests, coupled with the unprovoked mine attack on Republic of Korea (ROK) soldiers in the DMZ last August, are the latest in a series of actions intended to destabilize the Peninsula, challenge ROK President Park's leadership, and raise tensions.

While the international community urges North Korea to live up to its international obligations and return to credible negotiations under the Six-Party Talks framework, Pyongyang has shown no willingness to seriously discuss denuclearization. Kim Jung Un is on a quest for nuclear weapons, and the technology to miniaturize them and deliver them intercontinentally. Additional nuclear tests are likely to occur. North Korea will also likely test and field improved mobile intercontinental ballistic missiles and intermediate range ballistic missiles (MUSUDAN) capable of reaching Japan, and actively pursue its submarine launched ballistic missile development program. On 6 February, North Korea launched its second space vehicle in direct violation of several United Nations Security Council Resolutions, firing a complex, multi-stage rocket that also forms the basis of an intercontinental ballistic missile. North Korea announced its intent to conduct "annual and regular" drills to advance this prohibited capability. I have no doubt they will do so.

North Korea refuses to abide by the rules and norms of the international community and represents a clear danger to regional peace, prosperity, and stability. In the cyber domain, North Korea has lesser cyber technical capabilities than other states, but has already demonstrated them as a way to impose costly damage to commercial entities. This was demonstrated in the high-profile attack on Sony Pictures Entertainment. North Korea sells weapons and weapons-related technologies in conflict with United Nation Security Council Resolution restrictions.

<u>Chinese Military Modernization and Strategic Intent</u>: China's military modernization program is transforming its forces into a high-tech military to achieve its dream of regional dominance, with growing aspirations of global reach and influence. Given China's economic rise, the goal may be natural; however, the lack of transparency on China's overall strategic intent behind its military investments and activities creates instability and regional anxiety.

China's navy and air forces are rapidly fielding advanced warships and planes. Over the past decade, the Chinese navy has significantly increased in size and is much more capable in every way. Chinese forces are operating at a higher tempo, in more places, and with greater sophistication than ever before. Chinese shipyards are constructing China's first cruiser-sized warship, their first indigenous aircraft carrier, and many classes of patrol boats, frigates, and destroyers. Newer, more capable submarines continue replacing older ones. New fighters (including the "Gen-5" J-31), bombers, special mission aircraft, and unmanned systems give China greater air capabilities, lethality, and flexibility. These advances have been aided and accelerated by systemic technology theft, enabling China to skip decades of research and development and go straight into production. Finally, the People's Liberation Army (PLA) is undergoing dramatic reorganization to improve its command and control of joint forces.

China's strategic capabilities are significant. The JIN-class ballistic missile submarine (Type 094) carries the JL-2 submarine launched ballistic missile capable of reaching parts of the continental U.S. and represents China's first credible sea-based nuclear deterrent. New road-mobile intercontinental ballistic missiles provide more strike options and greater survivability.

In the maritime domain, China's Navy (PLA(N)) is increasing its routine operations in the Indian Ocean, expanding the area and duration of operations and exercises in the Western and Central Pacific Ocean, and is beginning to act as a global navy - venturing into other areas, including Europe, North America, South America, Africa, and the Middle East.

While China's actions are causing concern among neighbors in the region, there are potential opportunities. Its small but growing number of bilateral and multinational exercises suggests Beijing's greater willingness to interact with partners. Support for UN Peace Keeping missions is an encouraging sign of Chinese willingness to play a more active and constructive role in international affairs. My goal is to convince China that the best way ahead is through peaceful cooperation, participation and conformance in a rules-based order, and by honoring agreements made in good faith.

Territorial Disputes: The political and military dynamic in the East and South China Seas is changing, and tactical miscalculations between claimants present threats to stability and security.

In the East China Sea, tensions between Japan and China over the Senkaku Islands continue. China seeks to challenge Japan's administrative control over the islands by deploying warships into the area, sailing coast guard ships inside the territorial waters surrounding the Senkakus, and intercepting Japanese reconnaissance flights. In April of 2014, President Obama affirmed that Article V of the U.S.-Japan Security Treaty includes the Senkaku Islands. I am bound to protect that promise.

In the South China Sea, the situation is more complex. There are six claimants to disputed features: Brunei, China, Malaysia, the Philippines, Taiwan, and Vietnam, and there are three notable disputes over territorial sovereignty. The first dispute is between China, Taiwan, and Vietnam over the sovereignty of the Paracel Islands, which China took by force from Vietnam and has occupied since 1974. The second dispute is between China, Taiwan, and the Philippines over Scarborough Reef, of which China seized control in 2012. The third dispute involves multiple claimants within the Spratly Islands where China, Taiwan, Vietnam, Brunei, Malaysia, and the Philippines each claim sovereignty over various features.

The U.S. takes no position on competing sovereignty claims in the South China Sea, but we encourage all countries to uphold international law, as reflected in the Law of the Sea Convention, which ensures unimpeded lawful commerce, freedom of navigation and overflight, and peaceful dispute resolution.

While China has not clearly defined the scope of its maritime claims in the South China Sea, China has unilaterally changed the status quo. Chinese leaders seem to believe that, through coercion, intimidation, and force, they can bypass accepted methods of dispute resolution. They have demonstrated this through aggressive artificial island building, and by growing a fleet of "white hull" ships and fishing vessels whose purpose is to dominate the area without the appearance of overt military force. China is now turning its artificial island projects into operating bases for forward-staging military capabilities - under the rubric of being civilian facilities. For example in January 2016, China landed civilian aircraft on its man-made airbase at Fiery Cross Reef. The PLA is installing new or improved radars, communications systems, and other military capabilities at seven separate reclaimed bases. The scale and scope of these projects are inconsistent with the China's stated purpose of supporting fishermen, commercial shipping, and search and rescue. Although Vietnam, Malaysia, the Philippines, and Taiwan have also conducted land reclamation in the South China Sea, their total - approximately 115 acres over 45 years - is dwarfed by the size, scope, speed, and scale of China's massive buildup. In a little over two years, China has constructed more than 3,000 acres of artificial land - heightening environmental concerns by destroying the fragile ecosystem of the South China Sea. Professor John McManus of the University of Miami has called this the most rapid rate of permanent loss of coral reef area in human history. Equally concerning is Beijing's repeated pronouncements that it will not accept any decision issued by the arbitral tribunal in the case filed by the Philippines under the Law of the Sea Convention..

China's actions undermine the international rules-based order. Furthermore, these actions have driven China's South China Sea neighbors to expand their own military capabilities and seek stronger relationships with the U.S. and one another. The result is a situation that is ripe for miscalculation that could escalate to conflicts that no one wants, in an area vital to global prosperity.

While preventing conflict in South China Sea requires patience and transparency among all parties, time favors the Chinese. For the U.S. to continue to play a constructive role in preventing conflict and supporting peaceful dispute resolution requires national resolve and a willingness to apply all elements of national power in the right measure to influence all claimants to use international dispute resolution mechanisms. For example, USPACOM recently conducted freedom of navigation operations in the South China Sea- the continuation of a longstanding U.S. practice. These operations are an important military tool to demonstrate America's commitment to the rule of law, including the fundamental concept of freedom of navigation. The U.S. will sail, fly, and operate wherever international law allows.

Russian Assertiveness: Though focused on Europe and the Middle East, Russia is engaged politically and militarily in the Indo-Asia-Pacific. Russian activity is assertive, but not confrontational. Ships and submarines of the Russian Pacific Fleet and long range aircraft routinely demonstrate Russia's message that it is a Pacific power.

Russian ballistic missile and attack submarines remain especially active in the region. The arrival in late 2015 of Russia's newest class of nuclear ballistic missile submarine (DOLGORUKIY SSBN) in the Far East is part of a modernization program for the Russian Pacific Fleet and signals the seriousness with which Moscow views this region.

Violent Extremism / Foreign Fighters: The Indo-Asia-Pacific has the largest Muslim population on the planet and extremism is a rising challenge. Of the many extremist groups in the Indo-Asia-Pacific, those connected to Islamic State of Iraq and the Levant (ISIL) or Al-Qa'ida (AQ) are of greatest concern. Foreign fighters from the Indo-Asia-Pacific have contributed to violence in Syria and Iraq and pose a growing threat to security in their home countries upon their return. Attacks in Australia and Bangladesh underscore regional concerns about self-radicalized actors. Small but growing numbers of Bangladeshi, Indonesian, and Philippine extremists have pledged fealty to ISIL, and threats to host nation and Western interests are rising. USPACOM - in coordination with USSOCOM - and partner nations are focused on disrupting these extremist networks.

Transnational Crime: Transnational Criminal Organizations (TCOs), many operating sophisticated global enterprises that traffic in human beings, weapons, drugs, and other illicit substances, exist throughout the Indo-Asia-Pacific. The revenue from criminal endeavors threatens stability and undermines human rights. Corruption follows wherever these organizations flourish, weakening governments and contributing to regional instability.

Methamphetamine and amphetamine-type stimulants continue to be the primary drug threat in the region. Joint Interagency Task Force-West (JIATF-W) reports that at least 90 percent of the precursor chemical seizures potentially destined for illicit methamphetamine production originates in China. Maritime container shipments of China-sourced chemicals are diverted for methamphetamine and heroin/opioid production in Mexico - a direct threat to the U.S. homeland. The Asia-Pacific is also a growing, lucrative market for illicit narcotics produced in the Western Hemisphere. Just last week, JIATF-W coordinated with French authorities in French Polynesia to apprehend a sailing vessel located with almost 750 kilograms of cocaine.

Nearly 36 million victims of human trafficking are estimated worldwide and nearly two-thirds are from Asia. Women and children - especially those from the lowest socioeconomic sectors - are the most vulnerable. Roughly half of those 36 million victims end up in the commercial sex trade, while others are forced into difficult and dangerous positions in factories, farms, as child soldiers, or as domestic servants. While much remains to be done, USPACOM forces, including JIATF-W, are building partner capacity and sharing intelligence in order to combat these transnational threats.

Proliferation Issues: The Indo-Asia-Pacific region has the busiest maritime and air ports in the world. Developing technology has outpaced many nations' ability to effectively manage export controls. Trade includes dual-use technology - commercial items controlled by the nuclear, ballistic missile, and chemical/biological weapons control regimes, including manufactured or re-exported materials from other nations with limited export control enforcement.

USPACOM's Countering Weapons of Mass Destruction (CWMD) community supports counter-proliferation operations throughout the Indo-Asia-Pacific region. USPACOM addresses concerns through key leader engagements, combined and joint exercises, and international security exchanges focused on counter proliferation activities. Recent success stories include Vietnam joining 104 nations as an endorsee of the Proliferation Security Initiative (PSI). The PSI rotational exercise series provides a framework for partner nations to improve legal authorities and operational capabilities to interdict WMD, delivery systems, and other related materials. Proactive dialogue under PSI is vital to reducing WMD proliferation.

USPACOM works with the Armed Forces of the Philippines to enhance military to military interoperability and provide assistance to military first responders' capability to respond to a WMD. Under section 1204 of the FY14 National Defense Authorization Act (NDAA), the primary objective of USPACOM's WMD assistance is to train and equip first responders. In Aug 2015, USPACOM, Service Components, and combat support agencies such as the Defense Threat Reduction Agency provided the Armed Forces of the Philippines (AFP) a "first class" Chemical, Biological, Radiation, Nuclear (CBRN) Defense capability. Under these section 1204 authorities, USPACOM will begin to work with Thailand, Vietnam, and Malaysia to enhance their capacity to respond to a WMD event.

Natural Disasters: The Indo-Asia-Pacific remains the world's most disaster-prone region, experiencing over 2,700 disasters that affected nearly 1.6 billion people in the past decade alone. In addition to seismic and weather disasters, areas of large populations, dense living conditions, and poor sanitation in the region create optimal conditions for the rapid spread of diseases. U.S. forces regularly train with allies and partners in disaster relief operations and are called upon often to respond to tragic events.

USPACOM's Center for Excellence for Disaster Management (CFE-DM) increases regional governments' readiness to respond to natural disasters by developing lessons learned and providing best practices. Many of the lessons learned and preparedness measures implemented after Typhoon Haiyan (Operation Damayan, November 2013) reduced damage and loss of life when Typhoon Hagupit struck the Philippines in 2014. To help USPACOM rapidly respond to future natural disasters, Vietnam is allowing sets of vehicles, equipment, and supplies to be prepositioned within its borders for disaster preparedness purposes. USPACOM will continue improving pre-crisis preparedness and working with allies and partners to improve responses whenever disasters strike, but it is important to note that disaster preparedness cannot overtake traditional military readiness as our focus.

Strategic Force Posture in the Indo-Asia-Pacific

The tyranny of distance and short indications and warnings timelines place a premium on robust, modern, and agile forward-stationed forces at high levels of readiness. USPACOM requires a force posture that credibly communicates U.S. resolve, strengthens alliances and partnerships, prevents conflict, and in the event of crisis, responds rapidly across the full range of military operations. USPACOM's strategic force posture is also supported by the deployment of rotational forces and the fielding of new capabilities and concepts that address operational shortfalls and critical gaps.

Global Force Management (GFM): In support of the Rebalance, the Department has undertaken GFM initiatives that include the deployment of Littoral Combat Ships to Singapore, replacing the aircraft carrier USS GEORGE WASHINGTON in Japan with the more capable USS RONALD REAGAN, the deployment of two additional ballistic missile defense-capable surface ships to Japan, and the stationing of additional submarines and a submarine tender in Guam. The Air Force deploys a broad range of aircraft as part of its Theater Force Package model including B-52s, F-22s, F-16s, E-8s, and RC-135s. The Army forward deployed a second ballistic missile defense radar in Japan, maintained a THAAD battery in Guam, and delivered training and presence across the region through Pacific Pathways, enhancing partnership opportunities without permanent basing. The Army also continues updating Prepositioned Stocks (APS) and advocating for the placement of Disaster Response activity sets across Southeast Asia. The Marine Corps continues to execute the Defense Policy Review Initiatives (DPRI), which will reduce the Marine Corps footprint in Japan and distribute Marine Air Ground Task Force (MAGTF) capability across the region. The Marine Corps is also expanding rotational presence in Australia through its Marine Rotational Force-Darwin initiative. USPACOM plans to improve rotational force presence in the Philippines via the Enhanced Defense Cooperation Agreement (EDCA) and establishing USAF dispersal capabilities in the Commonwealth of the Northern Mariana Islands (CNMI) and in the Northern Territory of Australia. Rotational forces west of the International Date Line are positioned to deter and defeat potential aggressors in the region. Finally, we are beginning consultations with the government of South Korea for the placement of a Terminal High Altitude Air Defense capability on the Korean Peninsula.

Posture Initiatives:
The size and scope of forward stationed forces and the challenges within the security environment require recapitalization and improvement to infrastructure in theater. To that end, fiscal year 2016 military construction projects largely reflect requirements that support fielding new capabilities in the region, to include the F-35 Joint Strike Fighter, CV-22 Osprey, C-130J Hercules, and F-22 Raptor. Additional investments support resiliency initiatives and infrastructure recapitalization in Australia, Guam, CNMI, Hawaii, and Japan; critical munitions throughput recapitalization in California (Military Ocean Terminal Concord); and quality of life investments for our forces in South Korea and Japan.

Additionally, USPACOM's force posture strategy seeks to provide the correct level of capital investment to support established posture initiatives and commitments, including efforts in Korea (Yongsan Relocation Plan and Land Partnership Plan) and Japan (Okinawa Consolidation and the Defense Policy Review Initiative). In support of these initiatives, the Government of Japan committed up to $3.1 billion to help realign U.S. Marines from Okinawa to Guam and other locations, and $4.5 billion to expand the airfield and associated facilities at Marine Corps Air Station Iwakuni. Korea and Japan maintain robust host nation funded construction programs, which play vital roles in supporting U.S. presence and enduring capabilities in the region. These vital partner contributions require the Services to program Planning and Design funds to ensure our allies deliver facilities that meet our requirements.

Furthermore, USPACOM is expanding its presence in various parts of the region to include completing the permanent stationing of THAAD on Guam, the addition of a submarine and sub tender in Guam, additional Aegis BMD capable ships to Japan, and seeking the assignment of additional Intelligence, Surveillance, and Reconnaissance (ISR) assets in the region. In support of the Rebalance, USPACOM is in the midst of executing four major Force Posture initiatives: (1) U.S.-Japan Defense Policy Review Initiative (DPRI) / USMC Distributed Laydown, (2) U.S. Forces Korea Realignment, (3) Resiliency Efforts, and (4) Agile Logistics.

- **DPRI:** USPACOM is making progress on DPRI/USMC Distributed Laydown initiatives; however, significant Japanese political challenges remain. Consolidation of U.S. Marines in Japan is dependent upon completion of Okinawa construction efforts to include the Futenma Replacement Facility (FRF). In spite of the Government of Japan (GOJ) political resolve and dedication of resources, progress on relocating Marines from Futenma to Camp Schwab is slow going. GOJ budgeted $258M in FY15 for 200 projects, but only 9 facilities have been completed with an additional 8 under construction. GOJ faces challenges in several areas, including overcoming Nago City obstruction impacting construction and controlling protester interference. The central government has dispatched police officers from the mainland to Okinawa to assist the Okinawa Prefectural Police in managing protest activity in and around U.S. bases in Okinawa. However, as of this writing, very little progress has been made in improving the situation and protests continue to escalate. While the issues in Okinawa continue, USPACOM made progress in laying the groundwork for relocating 5,000 Marines to Guam. Tied to the Guam effort, DoD is aggressively pursuing the establishment of the CNMI Joint Military Training (JMT) Area to mitigate joint training deficiencies in the region.

- **USFK Realignment:** The consolidation of U.S. forces in Korea via the Land Partnership Program (LPP) and Yongsan Relocation Program (YRP) is moving ahead at full-speed. Construction will triple the size of Camp Humphreys and increase the base's population to ~36,000 troops and family members. The ROK is bearing the majority of the relocation's cost, committing over $7.5 billion to the project. USPACOM appreciates Congress' continued support of DoD's largest peace-time relocation project.

- **Resiliency Efforts:** USPACOM resiliency efforts include investment in a more robust transportation infrastructure in ally and partner countries, mitigation of single points of failure via the dispersal and optimization of critical enablers, such as communication nodes, fuel, medical, and logistic support equipment, and hardening facilities. For example, USPACOM is hardening facilities in Guam and CNMI as well as enhancing airfields at dispersed sites throughout the theater.

- **Agile Logistics:** Due to time and distance required to move assets within the USPACOM region, it is imperative to invest in infrastructure to ensure logistics commodities - munitions, fuel, and other war materiel - are properly prepositioned, secured, and available to meet requirements. USPACOM continues to build capacity for pre-positioned war reserve fuel stocks and invest in munitions, fuel, and other war materiel facilities and infrastructure throughout the theater. For example, critical munitions throughput recapitalization in California (Military Ocean Terminal Concord) is necessary to support USPACOM plans and operations.

Readiness: USPACOM is a "fight tonight" theater with short timelines across vast spaces. Threats such as North Korea - which has over a hundred thousand rockets aimed at Seoul - require U.S. military forces in the region maintain a high level of readiness to respond rapidly to a crisis. USPACOM's readiness is evaluated against its ability to execute operational and contingency plans, which place a premium on forward-stationed, ready forces that can exercise, train, and operate with our partner nations' militaries and follow-on forces able to respond to operational contingencies.

Forward-stationed forces west of the International Date Line increase decision space and decrease response time, bolster the confidence of allies and partners, and reduce the chance of miscalculation by potential adversaries.

The ability of the U.S. to surge and globally maneuver ready forces is an asymmetric advantage that must be maintained. Over the past two decades of war, the U.S. has of necessity prioritized the readiness of deploying forces at the expense of follow-on-forces and critical investments needed to outpace emerging threats. A shortage of ready surge forces resulting from high operational demands, delayed maintenance periods due to sequestration, and training pipeline shortfalls limit responsiveness to emergent contingencies and greatly increase risk. These challenges grow each year as our forces downsize while continuing to deploy at unprecedented rates.

Fiscal uncertainty requires the Department to accept risk in long-term engagement opportunities with strategic consequences to U.S. relations and prestige. Continued budget uncertainty and changes in fiscal assumptions in the Future Years Defense Program (FYDP) degrade USPACOM's ability to plan and program, leading to sub-optimal utilization of resources. Services must be able to develop and execute long-term programs for modernization while meeting current readiness needs. Much of the supporting infrastructure in the Pacific and on the West Coast of the U.S. mainland was established during World War II and during the early years of the Cold War. The infrastructure requires investment to extend its service life but the Services struggle to maintain infrastructure sustainment, restoration, and modernization accounts at appropriate levels. If funding uncertainties continue, the U.S. will experience reduced warfighting capabilities and increased challenges in pacing maturing adversary threats.

Allies and Partners

USPACOM's forward presence, posture, and readiness reassure allies and partners of U.S. commitment to security in the Indo-Asia-Pacific. Strengthening these relationships is critical to meeting the challenges and seizing opportunities. Through bi-lateral and multi-lateral relationships and activities, USPACOM is building a community of like-minded nations that are committed to maintaining of the international rules-based order. The U.S.'s five Indo-Asia-Pacific treaty allies are Australia, Japan, Republic of Korea, Philippines, and Thailand. In addition, the U.S. continues to strengthen partnerships with New Zealand, India, and Singapore, and build new relationships that advance common interests with Vietnam, Mongolia, Malaysia and Indonesia. This year, USPACOM plans to leverage Fiscal Year 2016 National Defense Authorization Act, Public Law 114-92, Section 1263, "South China Sea Initiative" (Section

1263) authority, to begin implementing the Secretary's Southeast Asia Maritime Security Initiative (MSI) – an initiative Secretary Carter announced at the Shangri-La Dialogue that will increase the maritime security and maritime domain awareness capacity of the Philippines, Vietnam, Malaysia, Indonesia, and Thailand. The Secretary has made available $50 million in FY16 funding and announced an additional $375 million from FY17-20 to conduct MSI activities pursuant to this authority. MSI takes a regional approach to help our partners better sense activity within their sovereign territorial domain, share information with domestic joint and international combined forces, and contribute to regional peace and stability operations. I'm also looking forward to improving military-to-military relationships with Burma and Sri Lanka, once political conditions permit. Strengthening and modernizing alliances and partnerships is a top USPACOM priority.

Allies

Japan: The US-Japan alliance remains strong and operational cooperation between USPACOM and the Japan Joint Staff continues to increase. Our relationship is a cornerstone of regional stability. On September 19th, 2015 Japan's Peace and Security Legislation authorizing limited collective self-defense passed into law and will take effect this year. Japan's Peace and Security Legislation and the revised Guidelines for U.S.- Japan Defense Cooperation will significantly increase Japan's ability to contribute to peace and security. Japan's leadership has worked toward lessoning historical tensions and improving cooperation and collaboration with the Republic of Korea (ROK) in areas such as information sharing and disaster response The Government of Japan supports USPACOM activities to maintain freedom of navigation in the South China Sea. In another growing relationship, a Japanese destroyer participated in the U.S.-India-Japan trilateral exercise MALABAR in October and then transited the South China Sea in company with the USS Theodore Roosevelt in early November. Japanese P-3s exercised with the Philippines and operated in the South China Sea while returning to Japan from Southwest Asia.

Republic of Korea: The ROK alliance remains strong, and I am optimistic that the Japan-ROK relationship will continue to improve, which I hold as a top priority. The U.S. and ROK agreed to delay wartime operational control (OPCON) transfer and adopt a conditions-based approach, rather than following a calendar-based deadline. Secretary of Defense Carter and his counter-part, Minister Han, signed the Conditions Based OPCON Transition Plan (COTP) in November 2015 at the annual Security Consultative Meeting in Seoul. This is part of American and ROK efforts to modernize the alliance to better address continued threats and provocations from North Korea such as January's nuclear test and February's space launch. Trilateral cooperation with Japan is the next logical step to ensure both countries' mutual security.

Australia: The U.S.-Australia alliance anchors peace and stability in the region. Australia plays a leading role in regional security and capacity-building efforts and addressing disaster response. Australia is a key contributor to global security, contributing to counter-ISIL efforts in Iraq and the Resolute Support mission in Afghanistan. With the implementation of force posture initiatives, the Marine Rotational Force-Darwin successfully completed its third rotation while increasing its presence from 250 to 1,177 U.S. Marines. The fourth rotation begins in April 2016. The U.S. and Australia are increasing collaboration in counter-terrorism, space, cyber, integrated air missile defense, and regional capacity building. Australia is procuring high-tech

U.S. platforms that will increase interoperability. These include the F-35A Lightning II, P-8 Poseidon, C-17 Globemaster III, EA-18G Growler, Global Hawk UAVs, and MH-60R helicopters. To enhance synchronization and integration, the Australian Government provides a Flag Officer and a Senior Executive (civilian) to USPACOM and a General Officer to U.S. Army Pacific staffs on a full-time basis.

Philippines: The alliance between the Philippines and the U.S. has been important for more than 65 years. The Philippines Supreme Court recently upheld the Philippine's domestic approval of the Enhanced Defense Cooperation Agreement (EDCA) which will improve U.S. access and build Philippine military capacity by addressing capability gaps, long-term modernization, Maritime Security (MARSEC), Maritime Domain Awareness (MDA), and disaster response capabilities. USPACOM is exploring way to use MSI to realize Philippines MARSEC and MDA capability development. The Philippine Navy has made good use of two previously awarded Excess Defense Article (EDA) U.S. Coast Guard Cutters. During the 2015 Cooperation Readiness Afloat and Training (CARAT) exercise, one of the EDA cutters (BRP RAMON A. ALCARAZ PF-16) operated with the USS FORT WORTH, enhancing our shared security concerns. During the 2015 Asia-Pacific Economic Cooperation summit, President Obama announced the award of a third former U.S. Coast Guard cutter through the EDA program, which will significantly enhance the Philippine Navy's maritime security capabilities, and, through MSI, we are exploring ways to ensure that this vessel is delivered fully mission capable. U.S. P-3s and P-8s already operate from Clark Air Base on a rotational basis, and the EDCA will increase U.S. access in crisis to Philippine facilities that are important strategic locations. USPACOM provides information sharing and training for the Armed Forces of the Philippines in the areas of MARSEC and MDA, Additionally, USPACOM provided $3.5 million in Chemical, Biological, Radiological, and Nuclear (CBRN) equipment and two years of sustainment training to the Armed Forces Philippines Defense Initiative through the CBRN Defense programs. USPACOM appreciates the continued support of the Defense Threat Reduction Agency, Joint Program Executive Office, and Joint Requirements Office in providing CBRN equipment and training to partners in the region.

Thailand: The U.S. and Thailand's long relationship began with a Treaty of Amity and Commerce in 1833, now 183 years old; that relationship expanded into a defense treaty in 1954, and the U.S. continues to value our alliance and friendship. Unfortunately, the Thai military's ongoing control of the civilian government since May 2014 undermines this important relationship. The U.S. encourages a return to democracy that will fully restore our bond; until then, military engagements and exercises will continue in reduced form. USPACOM will continue demonstrating commitment to our oldest ally while also reinforcing democratic values and ideals. Moving forward, it would be my hope that we use MSI to more fully support Thailand's maritime security and maritime domain awareness capability as an important member of the region. Moving forward, it would be my hope that we use MSI to more fully support Thailand's maritime security and maritime domain awareness capability as an important member of the region.

Partners
Singapore: Singapore is our most important partner in Southeast Asia. It has been a major security cooperation partner for over a decade and provides invaluable access for U.S. forces.

The rotational deployment of Littoral Combat Ships to Changi Naval Base has been productive, and P-8s now operate out of Paya Lebar Air Base on a regular basis. USPACOM conducts dozens of military exercises each year with Singapore's Armed Forces, Singaporean military officers regularly attend U.S. professional military education, and Singaporean military personnel participate in advanced military training that is conducted throughout the United States. Singapore hosts the annual Shangri-La Dialogue, a Secretary of Defense-level event that deepens regional ties and tables important issues for discussion. The combination of forward deployed forces and deep training relationships contribute to readiness, build deeper ties, and allow the U.S. to promote maritime security and stability with regional partners.

India: The new found momentum in our bilateral relationship with India represents USPACOM's most promising strategic opportunity. In January 2015, President Obama and Prime Minister Modi signed a Joint Strategic Vision of the Asia-Pacific and Indian Ocean Region. This landmark document presents shared views and interests for the region. The U.S. / India military-to-military relationship deepens as forces increasingly train and operate together. USPACOM intends to add momentum to an important relationship. Through this end, I have made improving the military-to-military with India a formal Line of Effort at USPACOM. In June 2015, during Secretary of Defense Carter's visit to India, the U.S. and India renewed the ten-year Defense Framework Agreement. In 2015, U.S. and India militaries participated together in three major exercises and 62 other military exchanges covering scenarios ranging from high-end warfare to humanitarian assistance and disaster response. The US-India Defense Technology and Trade Initiative (DTTI) further expands opportunities. Defense sales are at an all-time high and U.S.-sourced airframes, such as P-8s, C-130Js, C-17s, AH-64s and CH-47s, increase interoperability. USPACOM will advance the partnership with India by expanding the scope of military-to-military interactions.

New Zealand: Despite differences over nuclear policy, our military-to-military relationship with New Zealand, underpinned by the Wellington and Washington Declarations, is on solid footing. The New Zealand military has fought, flown, and sailed with U.S. forces since the beginning of Operation Enduring Freedom. New Zealand continues to be a respected voice in international politics and a recognized leader in the South Pacific that shares common security concerns with the U.S., including terrorism, transnational crime, and maritime security. Military-to-military relations and defense engagements with New Zealand remain strong.

Vietnam: Vietnam's growing economy and their concerns over Chinese coercion presents a strategic opportunity for the U.S. to add another regional partner. USPACOM is moving forward with Vietnam to improve Vietnam's capacity and capability in maritime security, disaster response. We are also exploring ways to use MSI to support Vietnam's maritime security modernization efforts, including in the area of search and rescue. In addition, Vietnam has agreed to allow U.S. prepositioning humanitarian stocks and supplies for disaster preparedness purposes.

Indonesia: Indonesia is an important security partner in Southeast Asia. President Joko Widodo's initiative to transform Indonesia into a global maritime "Fulcrum" demonstrates Indonesia's desire to play a larger role in international diplomatic, economic, and security issues. Again, USPACOM is developing ways to partner with Indonesian security forces through MSI and other U.S. security cooperation programs to improve Indonesia's maritime security capacity and encouraging a collaborative regional maritime security architecture. Indonesia is not a claimant to territory in South China Sea maritime dispute, but it is reinforcing security on and around its Natuna Islands. Indonesia will maintain relationships with other influential nations such as Russia and China, but security cooperation with the U.S. is a top priority for Jakarta. As a tangible sign of this, the United States and Indonesia signed a ministerial-level Joint Statement on Comprehensive Defense Cooperation in October.

Malaysia: Malaysia is another important contributor to regional peace and security. Through the Comprehensive Partnership with Malaysia, the U.S. and Malaysia promote regional stability. Malaysia's regional leadership role, technologically advanced industry, stable economy, and capable military make it an important partner in securing peace and prosperity in Southeast Asia. USPACOM continues to assist Malaysia in building an amphibious force to address non-traditional threats in and around Malaysia's territorial waters. Malaysia seeks U.S. support in developing a more capable Coast Guard through the Malaysia Maritime Enforcement Agency. These capabilities and engagements demonstrate Malaysia's capacity and resolve to ensure regional and domestic security, and Malaysia develops opportunities for multilateral security cooperation through Cooperation Afloat Readiness and Training (CARAT) exercises. Like other Section 1263-designated countries, we are exploring ways that MSI can support Malaysia's maritime security requirements in each of these areas.

Sri Lanka: President Sirisena, elected in January, is serious about addressing Sri Lanka's human rights issues. We have an opportunity to expand U.S. interests with Sri Lanka - Asia's oldest democracy - and will proceed deliberately as progress is made. Given Sri Lanka's strategic location, it is in America's interest to increase military collaboration and cooperation. As conditions permit, USPACOM will expand military leadership discussions, increase naval engagement, and focus on defense institution building in areas such as demobilizing and military professionalism.

Others
In addition to Indo-Asia-Pacific allies and partners, USPACOM has many other unique relationships throughout the region with countries, jurisdictions, and international governmental organizations. These relationships are important parts of our overall strategy.

Taiwan: Free and fair democratic elections in January on the island of Taiwan reflect shared values with the U.S. The U.S. maintains its unofficial relations with Taiwan through the American Institute in Taiwan and we continue supporting Taiwan's security. USPACOM will continue to fulfill U.S. commitments under the Taiwan Relations Act; continued arms sales to Taiwan are an important part of that policy and help ensure the preservation of democratic government institutions.

The United Kingdom (UK), Canada, and France: Staunch NATO allies, the UK, Canada, and France are also Indo-Asia-Pacific nations, each with significant interests in the Pacific and Indian Oceans, including territories, allies, partners, and trade. Each participates in PACFLT's RIMPAC and other major exercises, and deploy ships, submarines, and other forces to the region for operational, partner capacity, law enforcement and disaster response missions. Canada has a

General Officer serving as a Deputy Director for Operations at USPACOM; the UK will assign a similar grade officer to serve as Director of USPACOM's Theater Security Cooperation effort. Each nations' leadership expressed renewed commitment to the region, and USPACOM welcomes and supports their efforts.

The Association of Southeast Asian Nations (ASEAN): While not a military alliance, ASEAN is among the most important multilateral forums in the region. The ten ASEAN member states, under the chairmanship of Malaysia last year and Laos this year, seek to improve multilateral security engagements and advance stability in the Indo-Asia-Pacific. ASEAN-centered political-security fora such as the ASEAN Defense Minister's Meeting Plus (ADMM-Plus) and ASEAN Regional Forum (ARF) have encouraged ASEAN members and China to conclude a meaningful, substantive Code of Conduct for the South China Sea. USPACOM investment in the ADMM-Plus, ARF and other U.S. ASEAN defense engagements improve multilateral defense cooperation and promote regional norms. Facilitating capacity building through incrementally increasing the complexity of ASEAN's recurring multilateral exercises is a priority. In 2016, USPACOM will participate in the second series of ADMM-Plus' three major exercises.

China: The U.S.-China relationship remains complex. While Chinese actions and provocations create tension in the region, there are also opportunities for cooperation. The U.S. approach to China encourages a dialogue between the armed forces of both countries to expand practical cooperation where national interests converge and to constructively manage differences through sustained and substantive consultations. USPACOM's engagements with China, governed by section 1201 of the FY2000 NDAA, improve transparency and reduce risk of unintended incidents, enhancing regional stability.

USPACOM executed over 50 bilateral and numerous multilateral engagements last year with China. USPACOM supports our national effort to encourage China to support the existing security architecture; however, China's base-building and militarization in the South China Sea, its lack of transparency regarding military modernization efforts, and continued malicious cyber activity raise regional tension and greatly hinder U.S.-China cooperation. Instead of jointly working toward reinforcing international rules and law to promote regional peace and stability, U.S.-China engagements are often focused on reducing friction and avoiding miscalculation.

USPACOM hosted a U.S.-China Military Maritime Consultative Agreement plenary and working group focused on operational safety in November 2015. USPACOM also provided significant support to the development of the Rules of Behavior memorandum of understanding on safety in the air and maritime domain. Ongoing dialogues led to improved communications and safer encounters at sea and in the air.

There are areas where U.S. and Chinese militaries cooperate in areas of common interest, such as counter piracy, military medicine, and disaster response. The most successful engagements focused on military medical cooperation and shared health concerns. For example, in January 2015, the PLA hosted the USPACOM Surgeon and component surgeons in Beijing, Xi'an and Shanghai focused on Disaster Response, Pandemic and Emerging Infectious Diseases, and Soldier Care. In September, the USPACOM Surgeon sponsored the third acupuncture subject matter expert exchange between U.S. and PLA acupuncturists in Beijing, leading to collaborative research on acupuncture treatment for post-traumatic stress disorder. USPACOM encourages China's participation in international efforts to address shared challenges in a manner consistent with international law and standards.

Bilateral and Multilateral Approaches: USPACOM is directly connected to regional leaders. I am in frequent communication with my regional counterparts and appreciate the ability to reach out at any time to share perspectives. USPACOM maintains a close link with allies and partners through staff exchange and liaison officers, in addition to a series of formal bilateral mechanisms. In Australia, key engagements stem from the ANZUS treaty obligations, guided by USPACOM's principle bilateral event with Australia, the Military Representatives Meeting. Similarly, USPACOM's military to military relationship with Japan is guided by the annual Japan Senior Leader Seminar. Military Committee and Security Consultative Meetings are the preeminent bilateral mechanisms that guide the ROK and U.S. alliance. Each year, USPACOM co-hosts the Mutual Defense Board and Security Engagement Board with the Armed Forces of the Philippines to deal with 21st-century challenges. USPACOM conducts annual Senior Staff Talks with Thailand to address security concerns and reinforce U.S. commitment to democratic principles. Bilateral mechanisms also exist with non-alliance partners throughout the region, including India, Indonesia, and Vietnam.

The future lies in multilateral security mechanisms. USPACOM is evolving key bilateral relationships into multilateral ones that will more effectively address shared security concerns. For example, US-Japan-ROK trilateral coordination in response to North Korean provocative behavior is improving. The ROK and Japan each recognize that provocative actions by North Korea will not be isolated to the peninsula and greater coordination and cooperation are required. The December 2014 signing of the US-Japan-ROK Trilateral Information Sharing Arrangement is an important step toward greater information sharing. This arrangement was first exercised in early January following the nuclear test in North Korea.

To encourage multilateral cooperation, USPACOM hosts the Chief of Defense Conference (CHODs) annually. The CHODs conference location rotates between Hawaii and a regional partner. In 2015, 31 countries attended the CHODs conference in Hawaii. USPACOM also participates in Australia-Japan-U.S. trilateral defense dialogues, including the Security and Defense Cooperation Forum (SDCF). The trilateral relationship between the U.S., Japan, and India is growing, as evidenced by the first trilateral ministerial meeting held last year. The U.S., Japan, and India share democratic values, interests in protecting sea lanes of commerce, and promoting adherence to international laws and norms. Next, USPACOM aims to build a powerful quadrilateral partnership framework of the most powerful democracies in the Indo-Asia-Pacific. India, Japan, Australia, and the U.S. working together will be a force for the maintenance of the regional rules-based order, counterbalancing and deterring coercion or unrestrained national ambitions.

Activities
Security Cooperation and Capacity Building: USPACOM's Security Cooperation approach focuses on building partner readiness, reducing partner capability gaps, and building partner capacity. One of the more powerful engagement resource tools is Foreign Military Financing (FMF). Favorable consideration for continued funding of FMF enables USPACOM to meet

regional challenges to include border security issues, disaster response, counterterrorism, and in particular, maritime security.

As I mentioned, USPACOM will leverage the FY16 NDAA section 1263 "South China Sea Initiative" authority to execute the Secretary's Southeast Asia Maritime Security Initiative to build maritime security and maritime domain awareness of partners in the South China Sea region, through assistance to, and training of, partner nation maritime security forces. USPACOM will continue to rely on FMF as a source of providing major end items to eligible countries. MSI support notified pursuant to the new Section 1263 authority should be viewed as complementary and additive in nature to these FMF plans. Under MSI, PACOM plans to provide niche capabilities, more multi-mission type of equipment, and connective tissue that will help partners better deploy and employ these maritime security capabilities, both domestically to protect their sovereign territory, but also as a means of fostering greater regional interoperability.

Maritime Domain Awareness: Southeast Asian partners have expressed strong enthusiasm and support for U.S. security cooperation efforts in the area of maritime domain awareness (MDA). USPACOM will leverage MSI and the new Section 1263 authority to develop multilateral approaches to information sharing toward a regional common operating picture. This year, the Philippines, Australia and the U.S. are co-hosting a workshop to discuss regional best practices. This civilian-military workshop will facilitate whole-of-government discussions on maritime challenges that support creation of a regional maritime domain awareness network to share information across Southeast Asian partners - another multilateral approach to addressing security challenges in the region.

Global Peace Operations Initiative (GPOI): Indo-Asia-Pacific countries provide over 40% of the world's uniformed peacekeepers to United Nations (UN) peacekeeping operations worldwide; half of those countries that provide UN peacekeepers are GPOI program partners. GPOI builds and maintains the capability, capacity, and effectiveness of partners to deploy professional forces to meet the UN's needs in peace and security operations. Partners are meeting program goals achieving, or making progress towards achieving, self-sustaining, indigenous training capability. In 2016, USPACOM and Mongolia will cohost a multinational peacekeeping exercise called KHAAN QUEST, training personnel from 37 nations for deployment to UN peacekeeping missions. USPACOM expects 28 regional GPOI partners in KHAAN QUEST. USPACOM will continue improving partner military peacekeeping skills and operational readiness and provide limited training facility refurbishment. Indonesia's plan to provide 4,000 deployable Peacekeeping Forces by 2020 is another opportunity for USPACOM to engage with Indonesian military forces.

Pacific Pathways: As an innovative way to overcome the Indo-Asia-Pacific's vast time-distance challenges, U.S. Army Pacific (USARPAC) created Pacific Pathways which sequentially deploys small units to multiple countries for training. Their forward presence also enables rapid response to humanitarian emergencies or regional crises. This cost-effective program ensures that our regionally aligned Army elements know how to deploy and fight in the Indo-Asia-Pacific alongside our allies and partners. I support and encourage this kind of innovative thinking, and it pays major dividends in both relationships and readiness.

Joint Exercise Program: USPACOM's Joint Exercise Program intentionally synchronizes frequent, relevant, and meaningful engagements across the Indo-Asia-Pacific region. This important program, funded through the Combatant Commander Exercise Engagement Training Transformation (CE2T2), improves readiness of forward deployed assigned forces. Exercises and training strengthen USPACOM's military preeminence and enhance relationships. USPACOM appreciates Congress' support for continued progress.

Pacific Partnership: U.S. Pacific Fleet's (PACFLT) Pacific Partnership is an annual disaster response preparedness mission to Southeast Asia and Oceania regions. Pacific Partnership includes participation from U.S. allies and partners to improve cooperation and understanding between partner and host nations ahead of major natural disasters that require a multinational response. Last year, USNS MERCY conducted a four-month deployment to Fiji, Papua New Guinea, the Philippines, and Vietnam and provided healthcare and surgical procedures, community health engagements, and engineering projects including nearly 700 surgeries, 3,800 dental exams, and 10 renovation and new construction projects.

Joint Enabling Capabilities Command: One organization that supports USPACOM's ability to respond rapidly and effectively to events in theater is TRANSCOM's Joint Enabling Capabilities Command (JECC). The JECC is critical to USPACOM's ability to facilitate rapid establishment of joint force headquarters, fulfill Global Response Force (GRF) execution, and bridge joint operational requirements by providing mission-tailored, ready joint capability packages.

Counter-Narcotics: The drug trade continues to grow and threaten stability across the region. It has become a massive business, with sophisticated global networks. USPACOM combats drug trafficking in the region through Joint Interagency Task Force-West (JIATF-W). Building partner capacity to counter illicit trafficking of narcotics continues in areas such as the tri-border area of the Philippines, Malaysia and Indonesia, the coastal areas of Vietnam and Cambodia, and the border regions of Bangladesh. USPACOM is also fighting illicit trafficking across the Northern Thai border in the historic "Golden Triangle" area and beginning new partnerships with France to combat trafficking in and through French Polynesia and the Southern Pacific. Counter-narcotics programs support law enforcement and security forces, enhance relationships with partner nation law enforcement agencies, and impede the flow of narcotics and other illicit commodities.

JIATF-W engagements with China are an essential part of the counter narcotics effort. Maritime container shipments of China-sourced chemicals are often diverted for methamphetamine and heroin/opioid production in Mexico - a direct threat to the U.S. homeland. As much as 90 percent of the precursor chemicals used in methamphetamine production originates in China. Further, the annual volume of methamphetamine seizures going into the U.S. exceeded cocaine seizures on the southwest border of the U.S. in recent years. Through a partnership with the Internal Revenue Service, JIATF-W leveraged Department of Defense counternarcotic authorities to open an additional avenue of cooperation with Chinese officials by providing anti-money laundering training to counterdrug efforts. These efforts show promise in improving communication, cooperation, and information sharing on significant criminal enterprises operating in the U.S. and China.

<u>The Daniel K. Inouye Asia-Pacific Center for Security Studies (DKI APCSS)</u>: DKI APCSS serves as a truly unique venue to empower regional security practitioners to more effectively and collaboratively contribute to regional security and stability. <u>This center is one of our asymmetric capabilities. No other country has anything quite like it.</u> Through its academic exchanges, workshops, and sustained alumni engagement activities, DKI APCSS helps build partner nation capacities and affirm U.S. interests in the region. DKI APCSS provides added support to the USPACOM mission in several uniquely focused areas: as one of the few organizations authorized to conduct carefully measured engagement with Burma defense officials; as the primary tool of security cooperation engagement with the Pacific Island region; and as USPACOM's lead in implementing the U.S. National Action Plan mandate to increase inclusion of women in the security sector under the Women, Peace, and Security program. Recent successes include development and implementation of a successful country-wide security plan for 2015 elections in Burma; building the capacity of government officials in preparation for the Lao 2016 chairmanship of ASEAN; enhancing the cybercrime investigation capability of the Bangladesh Police; developing rules of engagement for the Timor Leste police during peacetime; building a data system for collection of counterterrorism information in Vietnam; and improving coordination among Philippine national agencies, local government units, NGOs, and other stakeholders in disaster response.

<u>Center for Excellence-Disaster Management (CFE-DM)</u>: The CFE-DM is USPACOM's executive agent for collecting lessons learned and developing and sharing best practices to prepare U.S. and partner governments for disaster response. CFE-DM recently completed a Joint After-Action Review of USPACOM's disaster response to the April 2015 Nepal Earthquake (Operation SAHAYOGI HAAT). The success of the response is a testament to Nepali preparation and disaster risk reduction efforts that were enhanced by our ongoing training assistance. The civilian national disaster management structures functioned, and the initial international response coalesced around the Nepal Army's Multinational Military Coordination Center (MNMCC). Five years of USPACOM Theater Security Cooperation initiatives with regional partners, organizations, and international agencies facilitated this collaborative foreign disaster response. CFE-DM supports USPACOM's efforts to increase resilience and more effective disaster response capabilities.

Critical Capabilities

The most technical, high-end military challenges in the region are growing. While many improvements to posture, forward deployed forces, and our relationships help address these challenges, USPACOM requires the best, high-end warfighting capabilities available now and in the future. As Secretary Carter recently said about deterring our most advanced competitors, "We must have, and be seen to have, the ability to impose unacceptable costs on an advanced aggressor that will either dissuade them from taking provocative action or make them deeply regret it if they do." There are a number of mission sets and enablers that requires continuous focus and attention. These include undersea warfare, munitions, ISR, cyber, space, and Integrated Air and Missile Defense (IAMD) systems. We must preserve our asymmetric advantages in undersea- and anti-submarine warfare, and we must regain and retain fading abilities to counter anti-access / area-denial (A2/AD) strategies.

Today, China is "out-sticking" U.S. air and maritime forces in the Indo-Asia-Pacific region in terms of ranges of anti-ship weapons. I need increased lethality, specifically ships and aircraft equipped with faster, more lethal, and more survivable weapons systems. We must have longer range offensive weapons on every platform. Finally, we must have a networked force that provides greater options for action or response.

We face a significant A2/AD challenge in this region. Pacing the threat is not an option in my playbook. We must outpace the competition which requires continued investment in development and deployment of the latest technology to USPACOM. Examples include Navy Integrated Fires and the AEGIS Flight III destroyer and its Air and Missile Defense Radar (AMDR) – essential tools in the complex A2/AD battlespace in which our young men and women operate today. The arrival of the USS BARRY, USS BENFOLD and USS CHANCELLORSVILLE in the Western Pacific represent forward deploying cutting edge technology where it is needed.

Undersea Warfare: Of the world's 300 foreign submarines, roughly 200 are in the Indo-Asia-Pacific region; of which 150 belong to China, North Korea, and Russia. China is improving the lethality and survivability of its attack submarines and building quieter high-end, diesel- and nuclear-powered submarines. China has four operational JIN-class ballistic missile submarines (SSBNs) and at least one more may enter service by the end of this decade. When armed, a JIN-class SSBN will give China an important strategic capability that must be countered. Russia is a Pacific threat, modernizing its existing fleet of Oscar-class multi-purpose attack nuclear submarines (SSGNs) and producing their next generation Yasen-class SSGNs. Russia has also homeported their newest Dolgorukiy-class SSBN in the Pacific, significantly enhancing their strategic deterrence posture. USPACOM must maintain its asymmetric advantage in undersea warfare capability including our attack submarines, their munitions, and other anti-submarine warfare systems like the P-8 Poseidon and ship-borne systems.

Critical Munitions:. Critical munitions shortfalls are a top priority and concern. USPACOM advocates for continued investment, additional procurement, and improved munitions technologies to better deter and defeat aggression. Munitions are a major component of combat readiness. USPACOM forces need improvements in munitions technologies, production, and pre-positioning, but fiscal pressure places this at risk.

USPACOM weapon improvement priorities include long-range and stand-off strike weapons, longer-range anti-ship weapons (ship and aircraft-based), advanced air-to-air munitions, theater ballistic/cruise missile defense, torpedoes, naval mines, and a cluster munitions replacement. Our subsonic ship-to-ship munition, the Harpoon, is essentially the same missile we had in 1978, when I was a newly-commissioned Ensign. Nearly forty years later, competitors have developed supersonic ship-to-ship and land-based weapons that reach much farther, punch harder, and fly faster. USPACOM welcomes efforts to turn the tables back in our favor - quickly. In the air-to-air realm, USPACOM welcomes advancements in munitions that will provide an advantage in a complex air-to-air environment. Additionally, modernization and improvement to U.S. torpedo and naval mine capabilities and inventories are required to maintain U.S. undersea advantage. Continued improvements in the capability and capacity of ballistic/cruise missile defense interceptors will further enhance homeland defense capabilities and protect key regional nodes from aggressive action. In support of Korea, USPACOM supports efforts to acquire a replacement for aging cluster munitions.

Intelligence/Surveillance/Reconnaissance: The challenge of gathering credible ISR cannot be overstated, and it is a constantly evolving problem. The Indo-Asia-Pacific presents a dynamic security environment requiring flexible, reliable, survivable deep-look and persistent ISR to provide indications and warning and situational awareness across a vast geographic area. As previously noted, USPACOM faces a variety of challenges and potential flashpoints to include threats from North Korea, a resurgent Russia, an expanding China, terrorism, and territorial disputes. Several hundred thousand Americans live under a constant threat of attack by North Korea, with over a hundred thousand rockets able to range Seoul on little to no notice. These challenges require ISR to prevent strategic surprise and accurately assess the security environment and, if necessary, defeat potential adversaries. The Rebalance to the Asia-Pacific has increased USPACOM allocation of ISR resources. USPACOM will continue to require additional advanced ISR to avoid long-term risk.

Cyber and Space: The cyber domain, coupled with space, is the most likely "first salvo" in a future conflict. Increased cyber capacity and nefarious activity, especially by China, North Korea, and Russia underscore the growing requirement to evolve command, control, and operational authorities. I support a separate CYBERCOM functional combatant command that retains its "double-hatting" with the National Security Agency. I also believe that in order to fully leverage the cyber domain, USPACOM requires an enduring theater cyber capability able to provide cyber planning, integration, synchronization, and direction of cyber forces.

USPACOM relies on space based assets for satellite communications (SATCOM) and ISR across the range of military operations. The USPACOM region spans over half the globe and space based assets are high-demand, low-density resources. As the shared domain of space grows increasingly congested and contested, our adversaries are developing means to attack our space-enabled capabilities. USPACOM requires resilient SATCOM capability to support operations. China is pursuing a broad and robust array of counterspace capabilities, which includes direct-ascent anti-satellite missiles, co-orbital anti-satellite systems, computer network operations, ground-based satellite jammers and directed energy weapons.

Integrated Air and Missile Defense (IAMD): TPY-2 radars in Japan, the THAAD system on Guam, and the Sea-Based X-band Radar (SBX) based in Hawaii defend the U.S. homeland and our allies. USPACOM's IAMD priority is maintaining a credible, sustainable ballistic missile defense by forward deploying the latest in ballistic missile defense technologies to the Pacific. For example, the U.S. Seventh Fleet is increasing its Ballistic Missile Defense (BMD) capability with the addition of the USS BENFOLD, which arrived in Japan last year, and USS BARRY scheduled to arrive in early 2016. These ships received a midlife modernization, making them the most capable BMD ships in the world. The addition of these modernized ships enables the U.S. Seventh Fleet to better support the U.S.-Japan alliance with a credible ballistic missile defense capability. USPACOM continues to work with Japan, the Republic of Korea, and Australia to improve coordination and information sharing with the goal of creating a fully-integrated BMD architecture.

Innovation: Innovation is critical to addressing USPACOM's capability gaps and maintaining our military advantage. USPACOM partners with DoD-wide organizations, national laboratories, and industry to provide innovative solutions to fill capability requirements. In particular, USPACOM maintains a strong relationship with the OSD Strategic Capabilities Office (SCO), which is developing game-changing technologies for the Indo-Asia-Pacific. USPACOM strongly supports Deputy Secretary Work's Third Offset Strategy and the associated effort to strategically advance areas where the U.S. can maintain dominance. The ability to quickly and adaptively change joint operational concepts and innovatively employ current capabilities in a high-end fight is critical.

Conclusion

It has been over four years since the President announced the U.S. Rebalance to the Indo-Asia-Pacific. There is much more to the Rebalance than military activity and the success of this strategic concept depends as much on our economic and diplomatic efforts as it does on our military efforts. From the military perspective, I believe the Rebalance is working. This success is due in no small part to the support of this committee and the Congress. But we are not done, and we must not lose momentum. USPACOM appreciates your continued support. I ask this committee to support continued investment in future capabilities that meet the challenges in the Indo-Asia-Pacific. I appreciate your help in continuing to field the right numbers of existing capabilities. I ask for your support to our plans to adapt our regional force posture. Finally, I ask your continued support for our efforts to reinforce and enhance alliances and partnerships. Thank you for your enduring support to USPACOM and our men and women in uniform, and their families, who live and work in the vast Indo-Asia-Pacific.

Admiral Harry B. Harris, Jr.
Commander, U.S. Pacific Command

Admiral Harris was born in Japan and reared in Tennessee and Florida. Following graduation from the U.S. Naval Academy in 1978 and designation as a naval flight officer, he was assigned to Patrol Squadron (VP) 44. His subsequent operational tours include tactical action officer aboard USS Saratoga (CV 60); operations officer in Patrol Squadron (VP) 4 at Barbers Point, Hawaii; three tours with Patrol and Reconnaissance Wing 1 at Kami Seya, Japan; director of operations for U.S. 5th Fleet at Manama, Bahrain; and director of operations for U.S. Southern Command.

Harris commanded Patrol Squadron (VP) 46, Patrol and Reconnaissance Wing 1, Joint Task Force-Guantanamo, the U.S. 6th Fleet, Striking and Support Forces NATO, and the U.S. Pacific Fleet. Harris has served in every geographic combatant command region, and participated in the following major operations: S.S. Achille Lauro terrorist hijacking incident, Attain Document III (Libya, 1986), Earnest Will (Kuwaiti reflagged tanker ops, 1987-88), Desert Shield/Desert Storm, Southern Watch, Enduring Freedom, Iraqi Freedom, Willing Spirit (Colombia hostage rescue, 2006-7) and Odyssey Dawn (Libya, 2011). For Odyssey Dawn, he served as the Joint Force Maritime Component Commander afloat.

Harris' graduate education focused on East Asia security. He attended Harvard's Kennedy School of Government, Georgetown's School of Foreign Service, and Oxford University. He was a MIT Seminar 21 fellow.

Harris' staff assignments include aide to commander, U.S. Naval Forces Japan; chief speechwriter for the Chairman of the Joint Chiefs of Staff (CJCS); and three tours on the Navy Staff, including as an action officer in the Strategic Concepts Branch, director for the current operations and anti-terrorism/force protection division, and deputy chief of naval operations (CNO) for Communication Networks (OPNAV N6).

In October 2011, he was assigned as the assistant to the CJCS where he served as the Chairman's direct representative to the secretary of state and as the U.S. roadmap monitor for the Mid-East Peace Process. Harris was promoted to Admiral and assumed command of the U.S. Pacific Fleet in October 2013. He was designated as the Theater Joint Force Maritime Component commander. In May 2015, he assumed command of the U.S. Pacific Command.

Harris has logged 4,400 flight hours, including more than 400 combat hours, in maritime patrol and reconnaissance aircraft. His personal decorations include the Defense Distinguished Service Medal, Distinguished Service Medal (2 awards), Defense Superior Service Medal (3 awards), Legion of Merit (3 awards), the Bronze Star (2 awards), the Air Medal (1 strike/flight), and the State Department's Distinguished Honor Award. He is a recipient of the Navy League's Stephen Decatur, the CIA's Agency Seal Medal, the Ellis Island Medal of Honor, and APAICS Lifetime Achievement awards. He is the Navy's current "Gray Owl"—the NFO who has held this designation for the longest period.

**STATEMENT OF
GENERAL CURTIS M. SCAPARROTTI
COMMANDER, UNITED NATIONS COMMAND;
COMMANDER, UNITED STATES-REPUBLIC OF KOREA COMBINED FORCES
COMMAND;
AND COMMANDER, UNITED STATES FORCES KOREA
BEFORE THE
HOUSE ARMED SERVICES COMMITTEE**

February 24, 2016

TABLE OF CONTENTS

1. INTRODUCTION

Mr. Chairman and distinguished members of the Committee, I am honored to testify as the Commander of the United Nations Command (UNC), the United States–Republic of Korea (U.S.-ROK) Combined Forces Command (CFC), and United States Forces Korea (USFK). Thank you for your continued support to our Service Members, Civilians, Contractors, and their Families, whose service each day on "Freedom's Frontier" advances vital U.S. interests, strengthens the Alliance between the United States and the Republic of Korea, and makes a critical contribution to the stability of Northeast Asia. In my third year as the Commander, I have witnessed the U.S.-ROK Alliance grow stronger, as the Alliance has improved its capabilities, planning, and cooperation to counter evolving threats from North Korea and to advance our four priorities:

- Sustain and Strengthen the Alliance.
- Maintain the Armistice. Be Ready to "Fight Tonight" to Deter and Defeat Aggression.
- Transform the Alliance.
- Sustain the Force and Enhance the UNC/CFC/USFK Team.

Through this past August's land mine attack, North Korea's fourth nuclear test in January, and the TD-2 missile launch earlier this month, the United States and Republic of Korea stood united and resolute against North Korea's provocative actions. Our strength and combined actions are the product of established ROK-U.S. bilateral processes, the Alliance's shared commitment to remain ready to "Fight Tonight," and the alignment of American and Korean values and goals.

While the Command focuses on these core priorities, we are also looking to the future. The Alliance took concrete steps over this past year to enhance our ability to respond to North Korea's evolving asymmetric capabilities, strengthen ROK forces to lead the combined defense of the Republic of South Korea, and relocate U.S. forces to two enduring hubs south of Seoul.

2. AMERICA'S FUTURE IN KOREA – SECURING VITAL INTERESTS AND ADVANCING REGIONAL STABILITY

The UNC/CFC/USFK mission is vital to the broader effort to expand security and prosperity in the Asia-Pacific region. As a sub-unified Command of U.S. Pacific Command (PACOM), USFK's core responsibility is to deter and defeat external aggression against the Republic of Korea, which enhances stability in the Asia-Pacific region and affirms our commitment to the U.S.-ROK Mutual Defense Treaty. We cooperate closely with PACOM in its mission to promote security cooperation, encourage peaceful development, respond to contingencies, deter aggression, and, when necessary, fight to win.

From my perspective, the level of U.S. engagement demonstrated by USFK in Korea and PACOM in the broader region is critical in this time of opportunity and challenge in Asia. Expanding ties among Asian countries and across the Pacific have helped facilitate an era of robust economic growth and military advances. While these advances promote global expansion and interdependent stability, international tensions have risen from the actions of several regional nations' military modernization and the use of national power. In this context of significant and rapid change, the Republic of Korea's neighbors are adjusting their strategies to shape the region's future.

China's continued pursuit of its military modernization program and land reclamation activities have prompted concerns among many nations in the region. Even as China's relations with North Korea remain strained, Beijing continues to support the North Korean regime, remains its largest trading partner, and seeks to prevent spillover of North Korean issues.

Japan's decisions to take a more active role in its defense and to advance global security are viewed by many nations around the world as a positive development. Yet, some in China, the Republic of Korea, and North Korea have been critical, as historical issues continue to influence views on Japan's international role. In this complex setting, USFK continues to look for opportunities to advance trilateral military cooperation among the United States, Japan, and the Republic of Korea.

Over the past year, Russia has continued to expand its military presence, economic investment, and diplomatic engagement to reassert its strategic interests in the region. Russia conducted combined military drills with China in August, conducted multiple air patrols by its bombers throughout the region and into the Korean Air Defense Identification Zone, and named 2015 as a "Year of Friendship" between Russia and North Korea.

Unfortunately, North Korea has chosen not to embrace this era of change and prosperity, and has been omitted from many of the opportunities in 21st century Asia. Kim Jong Un, North Korea's singular leader and the third generation of the Kim Family, exercises complete control over the state and military decision-making process focused on preserving the survival of his regime. He maintains an extensive internal security apparatus that addresses any challenges to his rule and he has openly replaced several top military leaders to solidify his authority. Kim also perceives that the regime's survival relies on the domestic and international recognition of North Korea as a global and nuclear power. This January's fourth nuclear test and February's launch of a TD-2 missile configured as a satellite launch vehicle – its fifth long-range missile launch since 2006 – further demonstrate that North Korea will continue to defy UN Security Council resolutions and international norms in its attempts to seek the regime's desired recognition.

Similar to his father and grandfather, Kim has likewise demonstrated that violent provocations remain central to North Korea's strategy. For example, this past August, North Korea carried out a heinous landmine attack in the DMZ that grievously wounded two Korean Soldiers. Later in the month, tensions rapidly intensified with the deployment of additional forces to the DMZ, psychological operations, and hostile rhetoric which required a strong, yet measured Alliance response. Even though our combined actions enabled national leaders from the two Koreas to resolve the situation diplomatically, it demonstrated North Korea remains a credible and dangerous threat on the Peninsula.

We continue to assess that North Korea recognizes it cannot reunify the Korean Peninsula by force with its large, but aging, conventional military. While it continues to train and man its conventional force, North Korea remains focused on improving its asymmetric capabilities: nuclear weapons, long-range ballistic missiles, and cyber programs. In addition to its fourth nuclear test, the regime conducted a multitude of multiple rocket launch system tests, as well as no-notice Scud and No Dong missile tests from a variety of locations throughout North Korea. Upgrades continued on the Taepodong Inter-

Continental Ballistic Missile (ICBM) launch facility and development of a submarine-launched ballistic missile and vessel. Lastly, North Korea continued to improve its capabilities in the cyber domain which build on the regime's success of past cyberattacks.

Even as North Korea is investing heavily in asymmetric capabilities, its conventional military threats are still formidable. The KPA is the fourth-largest military in the world with several hundred ballistic missiles, the largest artillery force in the world with over 13,000 long-range and other artillery pieces, one of the largest chemical weapons stockpiles in the world, a biological weapons research program, and the world's largest special operations force. About three-quarters of its ground forces and half of its air and naval assets are within 60 miles of the Demilitarized Zone (DMZ). In the contested waters around the Northwest Islands and beyond the western end of the DMZ, North Korea has taken deliberate steps to strengthen its awareness and posture with additional navigation buoys, coastal observation posts, and naval patrols. These steps even include beginning construction of troop and weapon emplacements on Kal Do, an island less than three miles from Yeonpyeong Do, site of the 2010 North Korean shelling of the Republic of Korean military and civilian targets.

Due to these enduring and proximate threats, our Command must continue to deter North Korea's aggression as the risks and costs of a Korean conflict would be immense to the Republic of Korea, Northeast Asia, and the world. The region accounts for one-fifth of the world's economic output, 19% of global trade, four of the 13 largest economies, and four of the six largest militaries in the world. If deterrence fails, full-scale conflict in Korea would more closely parallel the high intensity combat of the Korean War than the recent wars in Iraq and Afghanistan. Furthermore, any conflict with North Korea would significantly increase the threat of the use of weapons of mass destruction.

3. THE COMMAND'S FOUR PRIORITIES – PROGRESS AND PROSPECTS

In the context of this unique strategic environment, the Command advances vital U.S. interests, strengthens the ROK-U.S. Alliance, and makes a critical contribution to security in the Asia-Pacific. This year, we have made progress on each of our four priorities – first, to sustain and strengthen the Alliance; second, to maintain the Armistice, while remaining ready to "Fight Tonight" to deter and defeat aggression; third, to transform the Alliance; and, finally, to sustain the force and enhance the UNC/CFC/USFK Team.

A. Sustain and Strengthen the Alliance. Three key innovations this year have led to substantive improvements in the ability of U.S. and ROK forces to operate together as integrated and capable allies.

1. A new ROK-U.S. Combined Division improves interoperability. For more than 60 years, the Soldiers of the U.S. 2nd Infantry Division (2ID) have stood shoulder-to-shoulder with our ROK allies. This year, that enduring commitment was taken one step further through the transformation of 2ID into a Combined ROK-U.S. Division. This new organization integrates over 40 ROK Army officers into the 2ID headquarters, fostering mutual trust, combined decision-making, and open communications. In addition, a ROK Army mechanized brigade will habitually train with the Combined Division's units to develop shared capabilities. If conflict comes to the Peninsula, this brigade will be under the operational control of the Combined Division to create a seamless capability.

2. Rotational forces improve readiness. In order to increase the effectiveness and readiness of U.S. Forces on the Peninsula, USFK rotates specifically selected unit capabilities instead of maintaining permanently stationed units with Service Members on individual one-year tours. Fully manned, trained, and mission-ready rotational forces also provide the Alliance elevated capabilities over time by introducing a greater number of the U.S. Service Members to the unique aspects of contingency operations in Korea.

In the summer of 2015, the U.S. Army began rotating Brigade Combat Teams (BCTs) into the Republic of Korea for the first time, on nine-month tours as the 2nd Heavy Brigade Combat Team (HBCT) of the 1st Cavalry Division arrived from Fort Hood, Texas. Just two months after the unit arrived, the BCT was able to integrate with the ROK Army to conduct a combined and joint exercise. 2ID's Combat Aviation Brigade has also increased its capabilities through the rotation of Aerial Reconnaissance Squadrons and the Counter Fire Task Force expanded it combat power by adding a rotational Multiple Launch Rocket System (MLRS) battalion.

Rotation of fully-trained and resourced forces to the Korean Peninsula is not just an Army commitment. The U.S. Navy's Pacific Fleet ships and aircraft routinely exercise in the waters surrounding the Korean Peninsula as part of their regular rotation throughout the Pacific. Furthermore, the U.S. Air Force rotates both Active and Reserve Component fighter squadrons to Korea, while the U.S. Marines deploy air-ground teams to exercise and practice interoperability with the ROK Marine Corps.

3. New capabilities improve the Alliance's defense and deterrence. The ROK government has continued to invest approximately 2.5% of its Gross Domestic Product in its national defense – one of the highest rates among U.S. allies. During this past year, the Republic of Korea made progress in enhancing future interoperable-warfighting capabilities by procuring upgrades such as PAC-3 missiles for the Patriot Weapon System, multi-role tanker-transport aircraft, and the AEGIS command and control and weapons system. These follow previous investments in F-35 Joint Strike Fighters, Global Hawk high-altitude unmanned aerial vehicles, and other important assets. Once integrated into our Alliance force structure, these systems will further enhance our readiness and capability. Additionally, we announced this month that we will begin bilateral consultations regarding the viability of deploying the Terminal High-Altitude Area Defense (THAAD) system to the Republic of Korea to upgrade our combined missile defense posture.

B. Maintain the Armistice. Be Ready to "Fight Tonight" to Deter and Defeat Aggression. The Command's focus on readiness proved critical to answering North Korean provocations this past year. Our cooperation affirmed both countries' pledge to develop Alliance solutions to Alliance challenges.

1. The Command deters and defends against aggression to foster stability on the Peninsula. President Obama noted at his October meeting with President Park that, from the events of this August, "North Korea was reminded that any provocation or aggression will be met by a strong, united response by the Republic of Korea and the United States." When crisis came, we were prepared. A constant focus on readiness and open communication enabled the Alliance to act deliberately and prudently. The Alliance's actions deterred broader North Korean provocations and set the stage for a peaceful resolution of the crisis.

2. Three successful exercises enhance the Command's readiness. UNC/CFC/USFK enhanced its readiness through its three annual multinational, combined, and joint exercises – KEY RESOLVE, FOAL EAGLE, and ULCHI FREEDOM GUARDIAN. KEY RESOLVE and ULCHI FREEDOM GUARDIAN are annual, computer-simulated command post exercises that focus on crisis management and the defense of the Republic of Korea. FOAL EAGLE is an annual field training exercise to ensure operational and tactical readiness. All three exercises provide realistic scenarios that prepare our forces, to include additional participants from the UNC, to deter and defeat North Korean aggression and potential instability in the region. They are essential in improving ROK-U.S. crisis management, combat readiness, and interoperability.

We also aligned USFK's readiness program on the Korean Peninsula with PACOM's regional efforts. In August 2015, USFK and PACOM integrated for the first time the Korea-based ULCHI FREEDOM GUARDIAN exercise and PACOM's PACIFIC SENTRY command and control exercise. This coordination allowed the Alliance to test effective decision-making and mutual support with PACOM.

3. A revitalizing UNC strengthens the international contribution to Korea's defense. Last year, we increased our efforts to further strengthen the engagement of the United Nations Command's 17 Sending States in our day-to-day operations. When North Korean aggression raises tensions, the Sending States provide credible and multinational support for the defense of the Republic of Korea.

To revitalize the UNC, we will continue to engage all of the Sending States to leverage their many capabilities for Korea's defense. A senior Australian officer on our staff leads a sustained effort to enhance Sending State engagement in UNC's work. The representatives of the UNC Sending States participate in our exercises, train with us, meet monthly with the Command's senior leadership, and assign top-quality officers to work in the Command. During the ULCHI FREEDOM GUARDIAN 2015 exercise, the Command greatly appreciated the 89 participants from seven UNC Sending States (Australia, Great Britain, Canada, New Zealand, Colombia, Denmark, and France).

C. Transform the Alliance. In 2015, the Command and the Alliance continued to adapt to face both emerging and evolving challenges.

1. The MCM and SCM reaffirms ROK and U.S. commitment to defense cooperation. Following the October meeting between President Obama and President Park, in which our two countries recommitted to a comprehensive and global Alliance, our senior defense officials met in November at the 40th ROK-U.S. Military Committee Meeting (MCM) and the 47th ROK-U.S. Security Consultative Meeting (SCM). They approved and agreed to implement a new concept to detect, disrupt, destroy, and defend (the "4Ds") against North Korean missile threats; pledged to address global security challenges of mutual interest; strengthened cooperation in the space and cyberspace domains; reaffirmed a timely completion of the Yongsan Relocation Plan and Land Partnership Plan; identified critical military capabilities that the Republic of Korean military must develop to meet the conditions of OPCON transition; and endorsed the Conditions-based Operational Control (OPCON) Transition Plan, or COT-P.

2. The plan for conditions-based OPCON transition (COT-P) defines an effective way forward. COT-P creates a well-designed pathway to implement a stable transfer of wartime OPCON of combined forces from the U.S. to the ROK. This Plan provides a road map for the Republic of Korea to develop the capabilities that will allow it to assume wartime Operational Control (OPCON) when the security environment on the Korean Peninsula and in the region is conducive to a stable transition.

3. Effective military planning positions the Alliance to respond to a changing threat environment. USFK regularly reviews and updates operations plans to ensure our readiness to respond to regional threats and crises. The combined ROK-U.S. operations plan has and will continue to evolve to enhance readiness and strengthen the ROK-U.S. Alliance's ability to defend the Republic of Korea and maintain stability on the Korean Peninsula.

D. Sustain the Force & Enhance the UNC/CFC/USFK Team. Our Multinational-Combined-Joint Force continues to foster a positive Command Climate and focus on the welfare of our team.

1. The Command fosters a positive Command Climate through trust and team-building. The foundations of our organization and a positive Command Climate consist of effective communication, trust, and teamwork. Regular training on prevention of sexual harassment, sexual assault, and suicides continues to be a priority. The result is a strong record of Service Member discipline in the Republic of

Korea. Over 99.4% of our Service Members demonstrate their discipline and desire to be law-abiding, good neighbors in Korea.

2. *Cohesive communities and new facilities promote Korea as an "Assignment of Choice."* This attention to the welfare of our entire team has been an important driver in making Korea an "Assignment of Choice." Our realistic training against a real North Korean threat, cohesive community, the safety of our host country, and the brand-new facilities at Camp Humphreys welcome members of our military to serve on "Freedom's Frontier."

4. CRITICAL NEAR-TERM ALLIANCE TRANSITIONS

Northeast Asia is one of the world's most dynamic regions. As a result, the Command's success is not only contingent on our ability to meet our immediate requirements, but also on our flexibility to adapt in the strategic environment to new opportunities and challenges. While we focus our efforts on our four Command priorities, we are also making decisions and taking actions now that shape the future of our Command and Alliance. Longer-term success requires both steadfast advancement of the Command's priority to maintain readiness to "Fight Tonight" and the agility to transform in the future.

A. Enhance the Alliance's capabilities. As the North Korean threat evolves, its extensive asymmetric arsenal could be used at a time and location of its choosing. This creates indications and warning challenges for the Alliance which require the United States and the Republic of Korea to develop new capabilities to detect and defend against this threat.

1. *Advance ISR, BMD, and critical munitions to sharpen our tools of deterrence.* Together, both countries must constantly improve their intelligence, surveillance, and reconnaissance capacity; develop a robust, tiered ballistic missile defense; field appropriate command and control assets; acquire necessary inventories of critical munitions; and enhance the tools to prevent, deter, and respond to cyber-attacks.

2. *The Tailored deterrence strategy underscores the U.S. commitment to the Peninsula.* We have developed and refined a Tailored Deterrence Strategy, which serves as a strategic framework for tailoring deterrence against North Korean nuclear and ballistic missile threat scenarios. By providing a full range of ready military capabilities, including the U.S. nuclear umbrella, conventional strike, and missile defense capabilities, this strategy supports deterrence and represents the U.S. commitment to provide and strengthen extended deterrence.

3. *The Combined Counter-Provocation Plan manages the risks of miscalculation.* We also have confidence in our Combined Counter-Provocation Plan. This plan improves our ability to respond to North Korean provocations as an Alliance, while managing the risks of miscalculation and escalation. The events of this August underscore how strong, yet measured responses set the conditions for diplomatic efforts to work.

B. Relocate the U.S. force in Korea. The Command made progress towards relocating the majority of U.S. forces in Korea to two enduring hubs south of Seoul – a Central Hub around the cities of Osan and Pyeongtaek, and a Southern Hub around the city of Daegu. The $10.7 billion program is the largest single construction program in the Department of Defense and is well on its way to realizing its goal of modernizing the warfighting Command in Korea, improving the Command's effectiveness in deterring North Korea, and defending the Republic of Korea.

1. *Construction peaks as workers build facilities to triple the size of Camp Humphreys.* At the end of 2015, approximately 65% of the program was completed. Currently, at the peak of production, workers are constructing 655 new buildings, and remodeling or demolishing 340 existing buildings to accommodate the increase in population from approximately 12,000 to more than 36,000 Service Members, Families, Civilians, and other members of our community. The majority of new facility construction at Humphreys will be completed in 2016, and the majority of unit relocations will occur through 2018. During these transitions, we are committed to making relocation decisions with the effective defense of the Republic of Korea as our most important priority.

2. *U.S. Naval Forces Korea moves its headquarters to Busan, collocated with the ROK Navy.* The project at Camp Humphreys is not the Command's only move. This year, U.S. Naval Forces in Korea relocated the majority of headquarters staff from Yongsan Garrison in Seoul to the ROK Navy base in Busan, to enable the two navy staffs to work closer on a daily basis. This is the first U.S. headquarters located on a ROK base.

5. USFK'S CRITICAL NEEDS

My top concern remains that we could have very little warning of a North Korean asymmetric provocation, which could start a cycle of action and counter-action, leading to unintended escalation. To remain effective as the threat evolves, we seek four critical capabilities:

First, **Intelligence, Surveillance, and Reconnaissance**, or ISR. ISR remains my top readiness challenge and resourcing priority as CFC/USFK requires increased, multi-discipline, persistent ISR capabilities to maintain situational awareness and provide adequate decision space for USFK, PACOM, and National senior leaders. Therefore, among various spectrum, deep look, and full-motion video (FMV) capabilities, I also request dependable Moving Target Indicator (MTI) support combined with an airborne command and control and battle management capability. The ability to correlate MTI with other airborne sensor data in near-real-time, with a robust on-board communications ability, contributes to a deeper understanding of the North Korean threat and intent.

Second, **Command, Control, Communications, Computers, and Intelligence**, or C4I. Both the United States and the Republic of Korea are investing in new tactical equipment that will comprise a reliable C4I architecture. We must maintain this momentum in improving C4I capabilities and interoperability, so we can communicate from tactical to strategic levels and between units in the field.

Third, **Ballistic Missile Defense**, or BMD. North Korea's missile program continues to develop, so it is critical for the Alliance to continue to build a layered and interoperable BMD capability. The U.S. PATRIOT system provides important defensive capabilities, and I have previously recommended to both governments that they consider a high-altitude missile defense capability. Meanwhile, the Republic of Korea is moving forward in the development of its Korea Air and Missile Defense (KAMD) and "Kill Chain." We have also made progress in advancing the interoperability of Alliance BMD capabilities, but there remains work to do in this area, particularly to further refine interoperability between systems.

Fourth, **Critical Munitions**. The Command has identified specific munitions that it must have on hand in the early days of any conflict on the Peninsula. In this phase, the Alliance relies on the U.S. and ROK Air Forces air superiority to provide time for ready forces to flow into the Republic of Korea. In order to ensure this supremacy through immediate Alliance capability and interoperability, we must have sufficient critical munitions on hand. Therefore, we will continue to work closely with the Republic of Korea to ensure it procures the appropriate types and numbers of critical munitions for the early phases of hostilities. Of note, the potential ban on cluster munitions could have a significant impact on our ability to defend the Republic of Korea.

With these capabilities, our Alliance will greatly improve its posture in Korea. If we continue to act together, with the consistent support we have experienced in both Washington and Seoul, I believe the Command and the Alliance will strengthen and ensure our capability to deter North Korea and defend the Republic of Korea and U.S. interests.

6. CONCLUSION

Over the past two-and-a-half years, I have seen steady progress in the U.S.-ROK Alliance. Last year, we were tested, and we found ourselves ready. Through annual exercises that rehearse U.S.-ROK cooperation, the commitment to readiness of U.S. and ROK armed forces, and our peoples' shared values and goals, UNC/CFC/USFK and the ROK-U.S. Alliance have successfully advanced our priorities and realization of our combined vision.

We are deeply thankful for the support of our Korean partners and the UNC Sending States. We appreciate and value the continued support of Congress and the American people, as it is your support that allows us to undertake this critical mission.

It is my honor to serve with the American Soldiers, Sailors, Airmen, and Marines and our government civilians who serve in the Republic of Korea. Their presence and actions ensure freedom and the success of our objectives. Finally, we would like to recognize the leadership and support of senior U.S. and ROK civilian and military leaders, Ambassador Mark Lippert, and Admiral Harry Harris, as we support vital U.S. interests, strengthen the Alliance between the United States and the Republic of Korea, and make a critical contribution to security and prosperity in the Asia-Pacific.

Thank you, and I look forward to our discussion.

GEN Curtis M. Scaparrotti
Commander
United Nations Command, Combined Forces Command, U.S. Forces Korea

General Curtis M. Scaparrotti is a native of Logan, Ohio, graduated from the United States Military Academy, West Point, in 1978, and was commissioned as a Second Lieutenant in the U.S. Army.

A career infantry officer, General Scaparrotti is the Commander, United Nations Command / Combined Forces Command / United States Forces Korea. He most recently served as the Director, Joint Staff. Prior to his tour with the Joint Staff, General Scaparrotti served as Commander, International Security Assistance Force Joint Command and Deputy Commander, U.S. Forces – Afghanistan, the Commanding General of I Corps and Joint Base Lewis-McChord, and the Commanding General of the 82nd Airborne Division.

In addition, General Scaparrotti has served in key leadership positions at the tactical, operational, and strategic level of the United States military to include Director of Operations, United States Central Command and as the 69th Commandant of Cadets at the United States Military Academy. He has commanded forces during Operations IRAQI FREEDOM, ENDURING FREEDOM (Afghanistan), SUPPORT HOPE (Zaire/Rwanda), JOINT ENDEAVOR (Bosnia-Herzegovina), and ASSURED RESPONSE (Liberia).

His military education includes the Infantry Officer Basic and Advanced Courses, Command and General Staff College, and the United States Army War College. He holds a Master's Degree in Administrative Education from the University of South Carolina.

His awards and decorations include the Defense Distinguished Service Medal, Distinguished Service Medal, Defense Superior Service Medal, Legion of Merit, Bronze Star, and the Army Meritorious Service Medal. He has earned the Combat Action Badge, Expert Infantryman Badge, Master Parachutist Badge, and Ranger Tab.

———————————————————

QUESTIONS SUBMITTED BY MEMBERS POST HEARING

FEBRUARY 24, 2016

———————————————————

QUESTION SUBMITTED BY MR. WILSON

Mr. WILSON. North Korea is seen as a technologically backward nation, and yet there is a growing presence of computers and other digital media devices that serve as a widow to the outside world. Do you see a way this be used to increase their awareness about the outside world, and help to break the information blockade their government tries to impose on them?

General SCAPARROTTI. As a result of increased electronic media in North Korea—including cell phones that number in the millions—outside information is indeed much more prevalent than in the past. Strong ideological campaigns backed by Kim Jong Un's documented and aggressive use of corporal and capital punishment, however, have limited the impacts of this outside information on North Korean society and leadership. Computers, in particular, are overwhelmingly tied to a nation-wide "intra-net" and cannot access the world wide web—only a few computers in select organizations have internet access. We do believe the North's leadership is concerned and sensitive to the type of information its citizens are receiving. It is indeed a regime vulnerability, albeit one Pyongyang has successfully controlled to date. Increased efforts targeting this vulnerability would add additional stress to the regime.

QUESTION SUBMITTED BY MR. SHUSTER

Mr. SHUSTER. You stated in the hearing that you would rely on two more battalions of Patriot if we "go to crisis" on the Korean peninsula. Do you believe the overall inventories of Patriot missiles and total number of Patriot battalions are sufficient to be able to deliver this capability?

General SCAPARROTTI. [The information referred to is classified and retained in the committee files.]

QUESTION SUBMITTED BY MR. CASTRO

Mr. CASTRO. You mentioned in your written testimony that the U.S. relationship with Japan is a cornerstone of regional stability. Can you speak to how we can further leverage our relationship with Japan to maintain peace and security in the region?

Admiral HARRIS. We further leverage our relationship with Japan to maintain peace and security through continued cooperation and support as they implement their national security strategy and legislative changes in the newly passed Peace and Security Legislation.

Japan's 2013 National Security strategy, their first-ever published strategy, emphasizes the need to make "proactive contributions to peace."

We welcome this approach by the Japanese and are cooperating with them to help them identify their priorities and coordinate with USPACOM and other partners (e.g. Australia) to complement our Theater Campaign Strategy.

For example, Japan is embarking on a program to "build partner capacity," especially maritime domain awareness capability and capacity for partners such as the Philippines, Vietnam, Indonesia, and Malaysia. Those efforts by Japan are complementary to our own efforts to help our partners manage their own security environment, and we are using venues such as security assistance synchronization/coordination fora to work together to maximize the benefits to countries like the Philippines.

Japan is very early in its process of executing its new strategy and building partner capacities. Our coordination and synchronization with them on this new strategy are also in the early stages, but Japan is making progress and we are learning how to work together to maintain peace and security in the region.

USPACOM will continue to encourage and support Japan in the conduct of presence operations throughout the region and, hopefully, we will see Japanese freedom of navigation operations in the future. As Japan looks to become more active in the theater, the regular presence of Japanese ships, aircraft and personnel operating in accordance with international law supports and reinforces our own messages about adherence to international norms, law and standards of behavior.

QUESTIONS SUBMITTED BY MR. COFFMAN

Mr. COFFMAN. Please describe the importance of space capabilities, such as communications, missile warning, and reconnaissance is to your mission. Related, to what extent are you concerned with our posture to adequately respond to the growing Chinese counterspace threats?

Admiral HARRIS. USPACOM relies heavily on space-based capabilities to conduct joint functions necessary in the execution of our OPLANs. Commanders at all levels rely on satellite communications (SATCOM) to command and control their forces and conduct Intelligence, Surveillance, and Reconnaissance (ISR) across the range of military operations. The USPACOM area of responsibility spans over half the globe and available SATCOM is a high-demand, low-density resource. Space-based intelligence, surveillance and reconnaissance (ISR) capabilities provide crucial intelligence data support to provide warning and enable targeting, force deployment and defense. Space-based positioning, navigation and timing (PNT), primarily from global positioning system (GPS), is fundamental to the maneuvering of forces and is a critical enabler for search and rescue efforts during peacetime and conflict. Finally, timely missile warning is essential to support active and passive defense of U.S., allied and civilian infrastructure and personnel.

As the shared domain of space continues to grow increasingly congested and contested, adversaries continue to develop means to curtail our access to space-enabled capabilities. I have significant concerns regarding China's continuing development and fielding of lethal and non-lethal counter-space systems, as these systems can threaten my ability to achieve OPLAN objectives. USPACOM requires resilient space capabilities to support operations. Resilience is achieved through careful consideration of the existing and required space, ground, and terminal segments of space systems to maximize flexibility and minimize vulnerability. As these threats continue to mature, the U.S., in coordination with our allies and partners, must develop and implement both material and non-material solutions to mitigate these threats.

Mr. COFFMAN. According to public reports, at a recent parade in North Korea, four missiles on KN–08 launchers were noticeably different than earlier missiles shown. Why? Are these the same missiles as previously seen or did we see in a new variant of these missiles in October?

Admiral HARRIS. [The information referred to is classified and retained in the committee files.]

QUESTIONS SUBMITTED BY MR. SCOTT

Mr. SCOTT. What additional resources do you need to dominate the cyber-battlefield? And, how would the creation of a Cyber Command enhance your ability to oppose technologically advanced adversaries?

Admiral HARRIS. To dominate the cyber-battlefield, USPACOM requires growth in the areas of cyber personnel, training, and tools. USPACOM requires additional personnel capable of conducting cyberspace operations planning and to effectively command and control the cyber mission forces operating in the Pacific theater. These personnel and the collective DOD cyberspace professionals require additional training in cyber intelligence, operations, and planning to better react to rapidly evolving cyberspace threats. Lastly, USPACOM requires additional tools such as a common operational picture capable of providing situational awareness for all three cyberspace lines of operation: DOD Information Network Operations, Defensive Cyberspace Operations, and Offensive Cyberspace Operations within the USPACOM area of responsibility. These tools would enhance my ability to create effects within cyberspace to counter the constant advancement of our adversaries' cyberspace capabilities.

I support the establishment of US Cyber Command as an independent combatant command. I believe this will enhance unity of effort within the department and accelerate the coordination and execution of global cyberspace operations.

Mr. SCOTT. In the wake of the nuclear test, what was the change in military relations between the United States and our South Korean partners?

General SCAPARROTTI. In short, the adversities we have faced since last August, to include the nuclear test, have revealed the strength of our U.S.-Republic of Korea (ROK) Alliance and made the Alliance stronger. Our military relations with the Republic of Korea (ROK) remain robust and agile as we coordinate in assessing the situation, consider Alliance options, close divergences through candid discussion, and as nations, support each other's national interests. Through these efforts, we have toughened our resolve to deter North Korea and improve our interoperable capabilities through combined actions that illustrate our Alliance strength. Extending beyond these actions, we continue to hold regular bilateral consultations at multiple levels, to include participation from other U.S. and ROK agencies, which further displays our combined dedication to deterring the threat and defending the Korean Peninsula.

Mr. SCOTT. What are the current gaps in your in-theatre intelligence, surveillance, and reconnaissance (ISR) capabilities with regard to North Korea? How does the Joint Surveillance and Target Attack Radar System (JSTARS) platform integrate into the current ISR network?

General SCAPARROTTI. [The information referred to is classified and retained in the committee files.]

QUESTIONS SUBMITTED BY MR. TAKAI

Mr. TAKAI. Building Partner Capacity: What is the United States doing to build up the naval power and MLE capabilities of Southeast Asian countries? Please provide specific examples.

Admiral HARRIS. Using Fiscal Year 2016 National Defense Authorization Act, Section 1263, "South China Sea Initiative" authority, the United States Department of Defense is planning to spend approximately $50 million this year to develop the naval and maritime law enforcement capabilities of the Philippines, Vietnam, Malaysia, Indonesia, Thailand, Singapore, and Brunei by investing in systems and training for those nations' navies and certain maritime law enforcement agencies. Congressional notification of specific capabilities is planned for March 2016 in accordance with U.S. law.

USPACOM has also made a number of investments in maritime security and maritime law enforcement in the Southeast Asia region using the DOD Counternarcotics Program. Specifically, there are three countries where USPACOM has ongoing efforts. First, in the Philippines, USPACOM has a long-running program in the Sulu Sea area to enhance the capability of the Philippine National Police Maritime Group. USPACOM provided extensive training and infrastructure development to expand the effectiveness of this element in policing the Sulu Sea area. In Cambodia, we have a multi-year effort underway with their National Committee for Maritime Security based in Sihanoukville, to expand their operational capability. Lastly, in Vietnam, USPACOM is in the beginning stages of program development with the Vietnam Border Guards to enhance their capabilities to combat illegal entry, transnational crime, smuggling and trade fraud.

Mr. TAKAI. Please describe the strategic and military/operational implications of China's deployment of surface-to-air missiles (SAMs) on Woody Island, in the disputed Paracel Island group. Do you expect similar deployments of SAMs, anti-ship cruise missiles, or other similar equipment to disputed islands in the Spratlys? What would be the strategic and military/operational implications of such deployments for the United States? What is your assessment of the potential military and law-enforcement utility of these newly expanded sites, both for China's asserting and defending its territorial claims in the South China Sea, and in potential conflict scenarios against U.S. forces?

Admiral HARRIS. [The information referred to is classified and retained in the committee files.]

Mr. TAKAI. What is your assessment of China's ability to use hybrid warfare tactics to gain control of small islands that are administered by another country? How might a hybrid warfare approach by China in the East China Sea and South China Sea create problems for the United States and its allies? What should the United States and its allies do to deter a hybrid warfare approach by China and to improve the options for responding in a contingency?

Admiral HARRIS. China has been using a hybrid warfare approach (blending conventional and irregular forces to create ambiguity, seize the initiative, and paralyze the adversary which may include the use of both traditional military and asymmetric systems) for years to incrementally increase its control over its South China Sea claims and to put greater pressure on other South China Sea claimants. It has been using a similar approach to challenge Japan's exclusive administration of the Senkaku Islands in the East China Sea. This is a whole-of-government Chinese approach that incorporates military and civil maritime forces, diplomacy, economic carrots and sticks, and legal warfare. If unchecked, this approach, I believe, will allow China eventually to be in a position through coercion or force to wrest control of the islands and features it claims in both the East and South China Seas.

This approach is a challenge to the U.S. and its allies because it demands a unified, whole-of-government effort to counter it. Military action alone will not be sufficient to counter a Chinese approach that is designed to achieve its goals while remaining below the threshold of military conflict. That is why coordination among the interagency and the strengthening of our alliances and partnerships in the region are so important.

Mr. TAKAI. Building Partner Capacity: What is the United States doing to build up the naval power and MLE capabilities of Southeast Asian countries? Please provide specific examples.

General SCAPARROTTI. I believe this question would best be answered by the Commander of Pacific Command and would respectfully defer to Admiral Harris's views on this matter.

Mr. TAKAI. What is your assessment of China's ability to use hybrid warfare tactics to gain control of small islands that are administered by another country? How might a hybrid warfare approach by China in the East China Sea and South China Sea create problems for the United States and its allies? What should the United States and its allies do to deter a hybrid warfare approach by China and to improve the options for responding in a contingency?

General SCAPARROTTI. [The information referred to is classified and retained in the committee files.]

––––––

QUESTIONS SUBMITTED BY MR. NUGENT

Mr. NUGENT. We know the Asia-Pacific is a key region for illicit trafficking of everything from counterfeit goods to narcotics to humans. How do you see illicit trafficking networks affecting U.S. policy interests in the Asia-Pacific region and what assets and capabilities do we have to tackle these threats? Additionally, are we seeing any indications that any of these illicit funds are being used by foreign terrorist organizations, or local insurgencies in places like Thailand or Burma, to support their operations?

Admiral HARRIS. Illicit trafficking exists to generate revenue for the traffickers. This distinction is primarily what separates transnational criminal organizations from ideologically driven terrorist or insurgent organizations.

I believe that how this revenue is ultimately used underlies a much larger national security issue. It isn't really about crime as much as it's about the ultimate stability of current global systems. These criminal organizations have amassed unprecedented wealth from illicit trade and they pose a significant threat. Drugs are still the foremost money-maker for criminal enterprises, but counterfeit goods of all types, endangered wildlife, and even human organs contribute to a massive, globalized black market enabled by technology, whose value even by conservative estimates would rank amongst the top twenty nations in the world by gross domestic product.

No longer do we simply have a counter-drug problem, we face an expanding, globalized, transnational crime problem.

Developing and transitional states offer the most fertile ground for growth of transnational crime and the nearly inevitable result is an intermingling of criminal and political power that sanctions corruption and undermines governmental institutions.

I see this corruption and associated instability as one of the biggest impacts on U.S. interests in the Indo-Asia-Pacific.

Instability is particularly visible in countries like Burma and Thailand, but exists elsewhere in the region as well. Countries positioned astride major drug trafficking corridors, especially those that also have disputed areas within their borders, are especially vulnerable to instability due in large part to the violence required to maintain these criminally lucrative areas. The illicit criminal networks formed by these elements are far reaching, transnational by definition, and between terrorism and crime is born more out of logistical convenience than any ideological convergence, and actually has its strongest overlap at the lower organizational levels. Various aspects of the criminal networks including travel facilitation, document fraud, and weapons procurement, help to meet the basic logistical requirements of terrorist, insurgent and criminal organizations across the region.

From a Defense Department perspective, the challenge is that we are tasked to fight and win the nation's wars—our authorities, our systems, our processes and our people were all built around traditional nation-state threats. Four of the five priority challenges listed in the Fiscal Year 2018 to 2022 Defense Planning Guidance are traditional state actors. The increasingly asymmetric threats from non-state actors, from terrorists to high-end criminals, continue to present new and unique issues for us. We must continue to creatively examine our approaches to defending the homeland using DOD assets and authorities such as the Department's counter-narcotics program.

My command remains actively engaged with partner nation law enforcement and military elements to counter these illicit activities and strongly advocates and supports regionally focused cooperation.

My approach to dealing with these issues really comes down to partnerships and international norms. I am focused on modernizing and strengthening our alliances and our partnerships, and we are working to advance international rules and norms in everything we do. All of our bilateral engagements and capacity building efforts are underpinned by these guiding principles. Whether we are working on information sharing with French Polynesia to enable successful interdictions of drug smugglers transiting Oceania, or building capacity with Philippine National Police to improve maritime security in in the Sulu Sea—we are committed to building a cooperative network of partners to help defeat these threats.